# Historic Flow Blue

## with Price Guide

## Jeffrey B. Snyder

Schiffer Publishing Ltd

77 Lower Valley Road, Atglen, PA 19310

# Dedication

To Sherry and Michael, my wife and son.

# Acknowledgments

I wish to express my gratitude to all the people who made this book possible. Dealers and collectors generously allowed me into their shops and homes, permitting me to disrupt their schedules and clutter their working and living spaces with a tangle of equipment. They made the photographs in this book possible. Experts all, these people were also free with suggestions and insights which enriched the text (and hospitality which enriched *me*). I offer my thanks to each of these individuals: Lucille and Norman Bagdon; Dorothy and Elmer Caskey, Trojan Antiques, Cynthiana, Kentucky 41031; Dorothy and Arnold Kowalsky; Louise and Charles Loehr, Louise's Old Things, Kutztown, Pennsylvania; Anne and Dave Middleton, Pot O' Gold Antiques; Joseph Nigro and Ralph Wick, Old Things Made New Again.

Copyright © 1994 by Jeffrey B. Snyder
Library of Congress Catalog Number: 94-65856

Printed in Hong Kong
ISBN: 0-88740-640-8

We are interested in hearing from authors
with book ideas on related topics.

Published by Schiffer Publishing Ltd.
77 Lower Valley Road
Atglen, PA 19310
Please write for a free catalog.
This book may be purchased from the publisher.
Please include $2.95 postage.
Try your bookstore first.

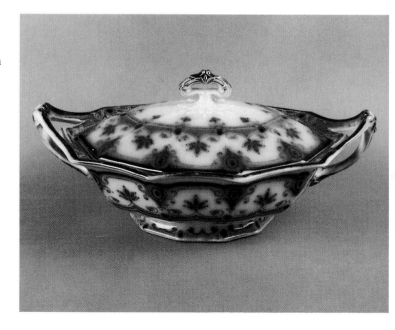

# Contents

England was the undisputed leader in the western world's ceramic market place in 1835. English potters had managed to produce earthenware ceramic bodies as white as the coveted Chinese porcelain but much more durable and eminently suitable for arduous overseas travel to foreign markets. These earthenwares were christened white wares, semi-porcelains, Spode's "Stone China" and Mason's acclaimed "Ironstone China." On the surfaces of these new wares England's potters placed striking mass-produced patterns quickly and inexpensively using transfer printing processes perfected in the eighteenth century in England. The quality of the blue printed wares was high. Large export markets opened or expanded in North America, Europe, and India where consumers sought elegant, matched sets of wares while avoiding the high costs and fragility of true porcelains.[1]

Transfer printing techniques allowed for the mass production of identical patterns in matching sets for the first time as seen with these pieces of a SHELL pattern tea set. The technique drew international consumers seeking elegant, matched sets of wares while dodging porcelain's high costs and fragility. Shell pattern creamer 5 3/4" high; waste bowl 5 1/2" high; teapot 9" high; sugar 7 1/2" high; cup 4" in diameter; saucer 6" in diameter. *Courtesy of Louise and Charles Loehr, Louise's Old Things, Kutztown, Pennsylvania.*

Among the transfer printed wares was the style which came to be known as "Flow Blue." These softly flowing prints and durable wares were popular in the American market from circa 1835 into the first quarter of the twentieth century. As the nineteenth century progressed, Flow Blue found its way into a variety of households—beginning with the well-to-do at its introduction, expanding to include the growing middle class by mid-century, and further expanding until these wares were available to nearly everyone by the beginning of the twentieth century.

The term Flow Blue broadly describes predominantly hard, white bodied earthenwares decorated with underglazed transfer printed designs. Once applied, these designs were caused to bleed or "flow" into the undecorated portions of the vessel. The addition of lime or chloride of ammonia into the protective shell of the fire-clay sagger surrounding the wares while firing the glaze produced the desired "flowing" effect.[2]

The transfer printing technique itself was a powerful tool for mass production. Perfected by Messrs. Sadler and Green of Liverpool in 1756, the process allowed a potter to quickly duplicate a pattern by transferring it from an engraved and pigment coated copper plate to a ceramic vessel via a specially treated paper. Transfer printing combined with the new hard white English ceramic bodies opened and expanded overseas markets for England's wares by 1815.[3]

The first successful color used in underglazed transfer printing during the late-eighteenth century was deep cobalt blue. Cobalt blue was the mainstay of underglazed transfer printing by 1776. It was the only color known to withstand the high temperatures used during early underglazing and the color used on the popular imported Chinese porcelains which the British were determined to emulate.[4]

The flowing color in Flow Blue, originally sneered at by British critics within the potting industry but never-the-less attractive and popular with overseas consumers, was also an aid to potters. Spreading over the white surface of their wares, the color bleed hid a myriad of potting imperfections from poorly joined seams on transfer prints requiring several sections to bubbles in the body of the ware. This was wonderful for manufacturers as the Victorian ideal of the "perfect finish" was either great realistic detail and meticulous surface finish or the concealment of the methods of production used to obtain the finished result. Flow

The AMOY gravy boat and undertray display all of the attributes associated with Flow Blue. It was manufactured by Doulton in 1844. The gravy boat measures 9" in length and the undertray measures 8 1/4" x 5 1/2". *Courtesy of Joseph Nigro & Ralph Wick, Old Things Made New Again.*

The addition of lime or chloride of ammonia in the firing of the glaze created the flowing effect, covering the undecorated white body with a blue tint as in this CHUSAN teapot by Joseph Clementson. Produced circa 1840, this teapot measures 9 1/2" high. *Courtesy of Lucille and Norman Bagdon.*

In 1848, Herbert Minton aptly explained one of the difficulties facing Flow Blue potters, "It is well that you should distinctly understand that, as respect all FB [flown blue] patterns, we cannot, after taking all the pains in our power, guarantee that all pieces of a service should be exactly the same tint and color and degree of flow."[5] That is evident in these two examples of the CHINESE DRAGON pattern, possibly of either Francis Morley (1845-1858) or the Ashworth brothers — George and Taylor, who began production in 1862. Both potters availed themselves of the earlier Masons Patent Ironstone manufacturers' mark as they gained control of the company. Chinese Dragon pitchers with dragon handles, marked Mason's Patent Ironstone China, and measuring 4 1/4" and 5 1/4" high to the spout. *Courtesy of Joseph Nigro & Ralph Wick, Old Things Made New Again.*

Blue enabled manufacturers to meet the ideal with ease. In fact, some pieces were so heavily flown that the original pattern was completely obscured. As underglazing techniques improved, other colors were used to make flowing wares including puce, mulberry and sepia, but blue remained the most popular.[6]

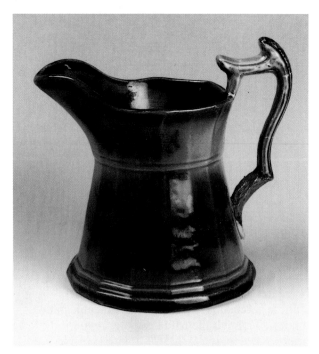

Manufacturers using transfer prints were able to produce more ceramics in less time at a lower cost than they had been able to make with hand decorating techniques. Only semi-skilled labor was required to apply the prints. The real artistry was in the hands of the engraver. Large manufacturers were able to hire their own engraver, while smaller potters relied on engraving firms for their patterns. Engraving firms frequently sold the same pattern to many potteries, which partially explains the duplication of patterns seen between potteries producing Flow Blue. In the end, the quality of the printed art on Flow Blue wares depended on the standards of the firms producing it and the taste of the consumers purchasing it.[8]

Some pieces were so heavily flown that the original pattern was completely obscured as is the case with this early sixteen panelled CHAPOO creamer produced by Wedgwood, circa 1850. 4 1/2" high. *Courtesy of Joseph Nigro & Ralph Wick, Old Things Made New Again.*

In 1828 underglaze techniques had been developed to transfer black, green, yellow, and red enamels, creating prints with two or more colors. The process was expensive however, each color requiring its own transfer and a separate firing. The early deep cobalt blue color itself changed around 1845 when coarser synthetic blues were introduced. In 1848 multiple color underglazing techniques were further developed by F. Collins and A. Reynolds of Hanley, allowing three colors, red, yellow and blue, to be applied in a single transfer with only one firing. Green and brown were added in 1852. This process was used into the 1860s.[7]

Engraving firms frequently sold the same pattern to a number of potteries, as is evident in these TOURAINE pattern plates by: Top: Henry Alcock & Co., circa 1898, 10" and Bottom: Stanley Pottery Company, 8 3/4" *Courtesy of Louise and Charles Loehr, Louise's Old Things, Kutztown, Pennsylvania.*

As underglazing techniques developed, new colors were added to the reliable cobalt blue. HONG KONG pattern soup bowls with flanches by William Ridgway, Son & Company (circa 1838-1848). Under and overglaze techniques were both used in this case. 10 3/8" in diameter. *Courtesy of Dorothy & Arnold Kowalsky.*

Stanley Pottery Company, Longton, Staffordshire, England, printed crown with manufacturers' name and TOURAINE pattern name. The dating of this mark is ambiguous as Stanley marks were printed by Colclough & Company using the Stanley name from 1903-1919 and by Stanley Pottery from 1928-1931. The registry mark indicates a registration date of 1898. *Courtesy of Louise and Charles Loehr, Louise's Old Things, Kutztown, Pennsylvania.*

Another example of duplication, this time the pattern name has been changed while the image remains the same. The pattern of the single berry bowl on top was christened IOWA by Arthur J. Wilkenson, while the two below were designated BLUE ROSE by W.H. Grindley. Each measures 6 1/4" in diameter and 1 1/4" in height. *Courtesy of Dorothy & Arnold Kowalsky.*

Transfer printed patterns also frequently included printed manufacturers' marks placed generally on the bases of ceramic wares. These marks contained the firm's name, initials, symbol and location — or some combination of these. Often the pattern name is supplied with the mark as well. These marks are one of the best and easiest guides to identifying Flow Blue. However, as the popularity of Flow Blue grew, and especially as European and American potteries joined English potteries in production, so many manufacturers joined in producing such enormous quantities of wares that not all the marks now may be identified. Additionally, many small firms either saw no reason to use marks (as they had no name recognition value) or sometimes used marks which have never been identified because

of the short lifespan and limited production of the company. Also, be aware that a few firms printed the name they have given to the name or sh*ape* of the ceramic body rather than the *name* of the *pattern*. This may cause some confusion.[9]

Flow Blue and its patterns may be organized into three general periods of production: The Early Victorian period from circa 1835 to 1860, the Middle Victorian period from the 1860s through the 1870s, and the Late Victorian period from the 1880s through the early 1900s. The term "Victorian" is used loosely, bearing in mind that the formidible English Queen Victoria did not take the throne until 1837 and ended her reign in 1901. Pattern designs and themes change recognizably through each period with certain exceptions during transitional years. Generally speaking, in the Early Victorian period oriental patterns based on imported Chinese porcelains and romanticized scenic patterns were the norm. Through the Middle Victorian period, floral patterns grew in popularity while Japanese motifs were introduced to the Western public. By the Late Victorian period, Japanese, Arts and Crafts and Art Nouveau designs proliferated. Familiarity with these periods and trends provides general dating guidelines for any piece which catches your eye. More will be said concerning the historical movements and influences which inspired pattern designs over the years later.[10] (For more information concerning Flow Blue transfer printing techniques and dating methods see Snyder, *Flow Blue. A Collector's Guide to Pattern, History, and Values,* 1992.)

Transfer printed patterns frequently included printed manufacturers' marks such as this one by Myott, Son & Co. (Ltd.), Alexander Pottery, Stoke (1898-1902), Cobridge (1902-1946), and Hanley (circa 1947- ). It features the firm's initials, name, symbol, country of origins, body ware type and the pattern name CRUMLIN. This mark was in use by Myott, Son & Co. (Ltd.) from circa 1900+. *Courtesy of Dorothy & Arnold Kowalsky.*

This work provides a broad sweep across a wide variety of wares including lofty tea services such as this BAMBOO pattern tea set with a rococo style teapot, sugar, creamer, tea cup and saucer, and a waste bowl with gold trim. This set was produced by Samuel Alcock and the teapot bears a registration mark indicating the year of registry was 1843. *Courtesy of Lucille and Norman Bagdon.*

This work provides a survey of patterns, manufacturers and vessel forms within the framework of the Victorian periods listed above. Patterns which have not previously been presented and a wider range of examples are included for some of the patterns given only limited coverage elsewhere. Some of the patterns may be judged contentious; nevertheless, they have been included for consideration within the broad scope of Flow Blue. Here also are a wide variety of household wares from elegant tea services to everyday wash basins.

Included as well are everyday items such as this KIN-SHAN pattern ewer and basin by Edward Challinor & Co. The basin measures 13 3/4" in diameter and 5 1/2" high while the pitcher measures 11" high to spout. *Courtesy of Lucille and Norman Bagdon.*

This work also presented the opportunity to provide much more. Chapter 2 explores the development of the Flow Blue market in America, setting the ware in its Victorian surroundings. This "in situ" approach provides a real understanding of Flow Blue's popularity throughout the Victorian era and the events that motivated people to purchase and use it. Also discussed are the international exhibitions beginning in 1851 and continuing throughout the rest of the nineteenth and into the twentieth century. These exhibitions provided manufacturers with the dual opportunities to both present their wares to potential customers and to take notice of new pattern designs being presented, sometimes for the first time, from other corners of the world.

Chapter 3 surveys a number of the prominent manufacturers who produced the ware, first in England and later in America and Europe. Information concerning the years of production and the quality of the wares produced is provided both from a modern vantage point and through the words of several authors writing during the nineteenth and early twentieth centuries.

Indentification and dates for the manufacturers and their marks in the captions were found in several sources which are mentioned here rather than in the endnotes for expediency. English manufacturers and their marks were identified by Geoffrey A. Godden's *Encyclopaedia of British Pottery and Porcelain Marks*. American marks were identified by Edwin Atlee Barber's *Marks of American Potters* and Lois Lehner's *Lehner's Encyclopedia of U.S. Marks on Pottery, Porcelain & Clay*. European manufacturers were identified with J. P. Cushion's *Handbook of Pottery & Porcelain Marks* and Ralph & Terry Kovel's *Kovels' New Dictionary of Marks*.

*"Beauty in things exists in the mind which contemplates them." "*—David Hume[1]

## Britain's Rise

During the reign of Queen Victoria (1837-1901), Britain attained a position of world dominance in commerce, finance and transportation as it prospered through the Industrial Revolution. Propelled by world-wide British colonial and manufacturing empires, this island nation reached new heights of wealth and power. Import tarrifs, colonial holdings and the Royal Navy all protected the nation's interests abroad while the growing railways supported domestic growth in agriculture and commerce. The British Reform Movement was rebuilding the nation's infrastructure, revamping the political system and improving working conditions in England with new child labor laws. A growing security permeated the nation, exemplified in dual boasts of the era: "The sun never set on the British Empire" and "Wherever a British citizen is in trouble, the Navy will be there!" A third boast could easily be added: "Wherever anyone wishes to buy ceramics, the potters of Staffordshire will be there!"[2]

The potters of the Staffordshire district of England had ample reason to feel secure. Their quest during the second half of the eighteenth century for an earthenware with a thinner, harder and whiter body to compete with Chinese export porcelain had succeeded, producing several durable white bodied wares. Added to that, transfer printing techniques developed in the middle of the eighteenth century improved during the first half of the nineteenth century to become a powerful tool for creating beautifully decorated wares with minimal expense and great speed. Transfer printing also enabled potters to produce sets with identical decoration, a feat impossible in earlier hand-decorated wares.[3]

Transfer printing also allowed potters to produce sets with identical decoration, a feat never before possible in hand-decorated wares. The three nested sets of platters in CHUSAN, MADRAS and MELBOURNE patterns are perfect examples. Nested set, CHUSAN Platters by Wedgwood. 20 7/8" x 16 7/8", 18 1/2" x 14 7/8", 16 3/4" x 15 3/8", 14 5/8" x 11 3/4", 12 1/2" x 10 1/4", 10 1/4" x 8 1/2". *Courtesy of Dorothy & Arnold Kowalsky.*

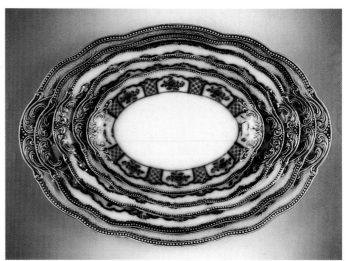

Nested set, MELBOURNE platters by Grindley, with and without gold trim, 18" x 12 3/4", 16 3/8" x 11 1/2", 12 3/4" x 9 1/4", 12 1/4" x 8 5/8", 10" x 7". *Courtesy of Dorothy & Arnold Kowalsky.*

Nested set, MADRAS platters by Doulton, 19 3/4" x 16", 17 5/8" x 14 1/8", 15 1/4" x 12 1/4", 13 3/8" x 10 5/8", 11" x 8 7/8", 9 3/4" x 8". Some come with gold trim and others without. Over the period of production, variations on thickness and weight occur depending on what was available during the run. *Courtesy of Dorothy & Arnold Kowalsky.*

When the inconveniences of the American Revolution and the War of 1812 were behind them, British potters set out to bolster strong connections with American consumers. This was not a difficult task as the demand for English ceramics was already strong. Long years of colonial rule featuring restrictions on trade from anywhere outside of Britain had conditioned Americans. To the chagrin of American potters, the popular belief was that English ceramics were by far the best. England's potters shipped to America deep blue transfer prints featuring American patriotic themes, famous personages, and well-known scenic views along with the standard fare of Chinese patterns. When these all were well received, other transfer-printed wares were introduced. By 1830 romantic views were replacing American scenes, and by no later than 1835 came Flow Blue.[4]

The positive effects of the Industrial Revolution that were improving production and distribution for English manufacturers were also at work in America. The new nation was rapidly changing from Thomas Jefferson's dream of an idylic agrarian society into a booming, boisterous industrial power. America developed a rapidly escalating number of consumers in the market for sophisticated wares which enabled them to quickly forget their agrarian roots.[5]

**America Before Mid-Century**

During the first half of the nineteenth century, Americans "tamed" enough of the eastern third of the continent to view the countryside surrounding their expanding cities and towns as "romantic". Long, rough-hewn hotels cropped up in favorite spots such as Niagra Falls, New York and Newport, Rhode Island to accomodate sightseers. This trend was in sharp contrast to earlier Puritanical images of the

wilderness as a place of dread and devils. In this new light, scenic views and idyllic Chinese landscapes seen through the soft lens of Flow Blue became popular, reinforcing the romantic ideal.[6]

During the first half of the nineteenth century, Americans came to view their rural surroundings as "romantic" countryside rather than as dangerous wilderness. Scenic views and idyllic Chinese landscapes reinforced the romantic ideal, especially when viewed through the soft lens of Flow Blue. AMOY plate by Davenport, circa 1844. 9" diameter *Courtesy of Anne & Dave Middleton, Pot O' Gold Antiques.*

Sightseeing became a popular nineteenth century pastime. This TIVOLI pattern by Thomas Furnival & Company seems the perfect embodiment of the idyllic trip to the country. The platter measures 17 7/8" x 14". *Courtesy of Dorothy & Arnold Kowalsky.*

Another reason for the popularity of a romantic image of wooded mountain and sandy shore may be traced to the actual dirtiness and difficulty of life in both rural and urban landscapes. Farms were dirty rugged places for anyone less than a wealthy gentleman farmer as may be expected, but the growing cities were far worse. Cities were densely populated, poorly drained and rarely cleaned. Streets were covered in thick layers of horse manure. In some areas people had not seen the road bed itself in living memory. Permeating the nostrils of every city dweller, regardless of position, was the stench of the slaughterhouses and the tanneries. Almost every city also had herds of free-roaming pigs. Charles Dickens wrote of New York's pigs in the early 1840s, "Take care of the pigs. Two portly sows are trotting up behind this carriage, and a select party of half a dozen gentlemen hogs have just now turned the corner... They are the city scavengers, these pigs."[7]

Flow Blue scenes and landscapes would provide escape from all this, temporarily. Gazing down into soft, clean views of exotic places with names like Hong Kong and Hindustan, urbanites and gentlemen farmers alike could dream of roaming in fantasy lands free of mud, manure and stench.

However, in this fertile soil, industry and opportunity grew rapidly. Factory villages rose around waterfalls or river rapids, each supporting from two to ten mills, mansions for their owners and superintendents, and rows of houses for the mill hands. Impressive manors and gothic cottages began to ring the larger cities as well, evidence of growing wealth with industrial innovation.[8]

Pristine Flow Blue scenes and landscapes offered an escape from the dirt and grime of nineteenth century life as well, particularly for the city dweller. HONG KONG covered vegetable dish, no manufacturer's mark. 6 1/2" high. *Courtesy of Anne & Dave Middleton, Pot O' Gold Antiques.*

Railroads began to wind their way across the landscape in the early period. Michael Chevalier, a French writer travelling America in 1838 noted "...there is a perfect mania in this country on the subject of railroads ... offering the ever-impatient Americans the service of their rapid cars at the points where the steamboats leave their passengers." Charles Dickens filled in the picture with gritty details in 1842,

"There is a great deal of jolting, a great deal of noise, a great deal of wall, not much window, a locomotive engine, a shriek, and a bell." With railroads came greater access to imported goods than had been enjoyed before. New markets opened, demand increased, lifestyles changed and trade in Flow Blue wares florished under these conditions.[9]

No herds of pigs, manure filled streets or foul smelling tanneries mar the exotic beauties of this HINDUSTAN patterned platter by John Maddock for the whistful Victorian daydreamer during a momentary escape from the gritty realities of nineteenth century life. The platter measures 15 7/8" x 12 3/8". *Courtesy of Dorothy & Arnold Kowalsky.*

## The Family Before Mid-Century

The social structure of family life changed in the nineteenth century as radically as the physical surroundings. Between 1780 and 1850 urban oriented wage labor replaced rural collective family labor. Men who had previously tilled the land side-by-side with their spouses and children were leaving for work outside the home. Where both parents and members of their close-knit agrarian communities had once raised the children, that role now fell solely on the women of the increasingly urban households.[10]

Married women came to rule over the affairs of the house while their husbands were away. A "cult of domesticity" developed repleat with manuals of social conduct, advice, moral lessons on women's roles within the family, and detailed examples depicting proper table settings and wares. As Chevalier described it in 1838, "The earnings of the man being sufficient for the support of the family, the woman has no other duties than to the care of the household, a circumstance still more advantageous for her children than for herself."[11]

As a result women were selecting furnishings and directing home affairs to an extent previously unknown. Women without children were also finding opportunities outside the home for income-earning work. This dramatically increased the resources of a couple and allowed them to purchase wares, including Flow Blue, that would have been beyond their parents' means in the eighteenth century. In England working women were placing the transfer prints onto Flow Blue wares. In America women were choosing to use them in their homes.[12]

Within those households before 1850, the most likely place to find pictorial art was on the dinner table and in the cupboards. Transfer prints, including Flow Blue, were providing thousands of homes with depictions of Oriental, European, English and American views where nothing but small wood cuts and engravings in books had been seen before. Only wealthy families hung pictorial art on their walls, and most of those were portraits.[13]

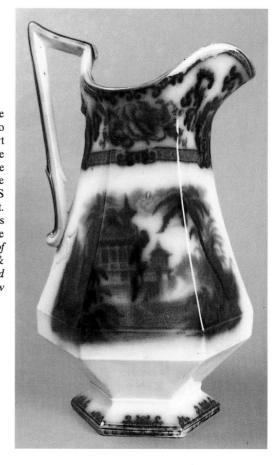

Prior to 1850, the most likely place to find pictorial art was not on the walls but in the cupboards or on the table. CYPRUS ewer by Davenport. The ewer measures 11 3/4" high to the spout. *Courtesy of Joseph Nigro & Ralph Wick, Old Things Made New Again.*

During the first half of the nineteenth century in America paintings to decorate the walls were scarce, even among the wealthy. Printed scenes on ceramics often filled the void. Flow Blue provided many homes with enticing idealized depictions of Oriental, European, English and American views including this GRECIAN SCROLL cup and saucer by T.J. & J. Mayer. Saucer, 6" dia.; cup 3 3/4" diameter x 3" high. *Courtesy of Anne & Dave Middleton, Pot O' Gold Antiques.*

A sponge-dish was part of the chamber set. The insert inverted as in this photograph held the sponge inside. Turned over, the insert became the recepticle for the wet sponge while bathing. MARBLE pattern sponge-dish by W.T. Copeland. *Courtesy of Lucille and Norman Bagdon.*

Another sign of a well-to-do family was the presence of a complete ceramic "chamber set" in every bed chamber, the latest advance in domestic sanitation. All but the most destitute had a couple of chamber pots to ward off nocturnal trips to the privy as the pots were available in a variety of English wares for low prices. However, full wash sets in each bedroom was the height of gentility, including a matching basin and ewer, a soap-dish, and a sponge-dish for private bathing, a cup for brushing teeth, a slop pail and a chamber pot with a cover to reduce disagreeable scents and spillage. Flow Blue wash sets produced by Minton, Wedgwood and other firms of all sizes were available. By mid-century chamber sets in every bed chamber would become more common and these sets remained a staple of the earthenware trade.[14]

The soap-dish was also an integral part of every chamber set. Keep in mind that the truly gentile would make sure their sets were all in the same pattern. FORMOSA pattern soap-dish. *Courtesy of Dorothy & Elmer Caskey, Trojan Antiques, Cynthiana, Kentucky 41031.*

A sure sign of a prosperous American family before mid-century was the prescense of complete chamber sets in every bed chamber. BLUE BELL wash ewer and face bowl, the face bowl was smaller than the body bowl. The ewer measures 7 1/4" high to the spout, the face bowl measures 9 1/2" diameter and 3 1/2" high. *Courtesy of Dorothy & Elmer Caskey, Trojan Antiques, Cynthiana, Kentucky 41031.*

Despite the best efforts of the woman in charge of the house, home life tended to be a gritty affair. Clothes were perennially sweat stained and stiff, both chamber pots and privies needed to be emptied and sanitized, all the more as the summer heat rose, and men chewing tobacco regularly created dirt and stains. Wherever a pipe smoker found it cumbersome or dangerous to smoke, he chewed. Tobacco chewing was very popular despite repeated complaints from women and foreign travellers alike. In the streets, barrooms, stores, and public transports chewers were unavoidable. In trains it was often difficult to find a seat or to look out the window as chewers spat their noisome juice everywhere. Similar problems arose at home. Spittoons were provided on trains, in some of the more particular establishments and in homes, but to little avail. Even if the chewer chose to aim for the spittoon, there was no guarantee he would hit it. Flow Blue spittoons are to be found, no doubt purchased by genteel ladies in the fervent hope that by some miracle the men who crossed their doorsteps would notice the well decorated recepticles and take aim.[15]

However, one of the most significant changes for many families from the eighteenth to the first half of the nineteenth century was their eating habits. During the eighteenth century it had been the custom for the average family to eat meals "in common" whereby a family sat down around a single bowl of food in the center of the table, each member armed only with a spoon. Everyone dipped their spoons into the meal, eating together from that one common bowl.[16]

By 1800 few families were left who practiced communal eating. Instead, most practiced individualized social eating, each member of the family having their own place setting and individual portions of food. In fact, anything that suggested the old communal ways was looked upon with disdain. English mass production techniques suited this change well, providing matched sets of dishes for everyone who could afford them.[17]

Very formal dinners with a superabundance of extravagant foods were not common during the first half of the nineteenth century for any but the wealthiest members of society. Limits as to what was served were set by the preservation techniques available during the period: underground storage, drying, smoking and salting. Few families saw regular supplies of fresh meat, and when they did it was only at the autumnal pig or winter steer slaughters.[18]

Victorian men chewed tobacco often and aimed infrequently when spitting. Spittoons were set out by housewives, businesses and railroads in the vain hope the vile juice could be contained instead of creating stains. Even when aiming chewers were notoriously bad marksmen, a fact noted with disgust by women and foreign visitors alike. Aboard trains there were often complaints about the difficulties of finding seats or looking out windows unstained with tobacco juice. These two spittoons in an unidentified Flow Blue pattern were hand-held models specifically designed to improve the aim by decreasing the distance. Each measures 8 1/2" high and 5 7/8" in diameter. *Courtesy of Dorothy & Arnold Kowalsky.*

During the first half of the nineteenth century, a meal-time ritual grew in the middle and upper classes. Elaborate rules of conduct requiring even more elaborate services surfaced. The great variety of form and decoration on Flow Blue during this period fit well with the new ideal of civil dining. Pedestaled sauce dishes in three pieces — base, lid, and bowl — by Ridgway, circa 1840-60. The pattern was not identified. The sauce dishes stand 8" high. *Courtesy of Dorothy & Elmer Caskey, Trojan Antiques, Cynthiana, Kentucky 41031.*

AMOY sauce tureen by Davenport, circa 1844, 8" x 8" x 5 3/4" high. *Courtesy of Joseph Nigro & Ralph Wick, Old Things Made New Again.*

AMOY platter by Davenport dating from 1836 as indicated by an impressed manufacturers' mark. 19 1/2" x 15". *Courtesy of Joseph Nigro & Ralph Wick, Old Things Made New Again.*

AMOY sauce and soup tureens with underplates by Davenport. *Courtesy of Joseph Nigro & Ralph Wick, Old Things Made New Again.*

AMOY covered hot cream pitcher by Davenport, circa 1844, measuring 5 3/4" high to the spout. *Courtesy of Joseph Nigro & Ralph Wick, Old Things Made New Again.*

AMOY covered vegetable and covered butter dishes by Davenport, dating circa 1844. *Courtesy of Joseph Nigro & Ralph Wick, Old Things Made New Again.*

AMOY "nut cups" by Davenport, circa 1844. 5 1/2" long. *Courtesy of Joseph Nigro & Ralph Wick, Old Things Made New Again.*

While large serving vessels and plates came and went, small items remained throughout the meal to reinforce a sense of refined dining. CASHMERE jam dish with an attached underplate, manufactured by Ridgway and Morley from circa 1842-1844. The jam dish measures 4 1/2" in diameter and 3 1/4" high. attached underplate. *Courtesy of Dorothy & Elmer Caskey, Trojan Antiques, Cynthiana, Kentucky 41031.*

A rare CASHMERE covered muffin dish by Ridgway and Morley, circa 1842. This muffin dish measures 10 3/8" in diameter x 6 1/2" high. *Courtesy of Louise and Charles Loehr, Louise's Old Things, Kutztown, Pennsylvania.*

Sure to make an impression was this large BLUE BELL pattern cheese dome, standing approx. 12" high. *Courtesy of Dorothy & Elmer Caskey, Trojan Antiques, Cynthiana, Kentucky 41031.*

Despite what was lacking, a meal-time ritual grew in the middle and upper classes with women's increasing sphere of influence within the home. Elaborate rules of conduct surfaced and with them even more elaborate vessels to be used during meals. This elaboration was reflected by an increase in decorative styles, in the amount of decoration on the wares, and the relative cost of ceramic wares used during a meal. The great variety in form and decoration on Flow Blue during this period fits right in with the new ideal of civil dining that needs may be met in an orderly and well-mannered fashion.[20]

Flow Blue found it's way into the kitchen as well as onto the dining table. An unidentified chrysanthimum pattern decorated treacle jar with a screw on lid. Prior to the introduction of granulated sugar, the sugarloaf made preparing cakes and desserts cumbersome. Treacle, a heavy molasses, was a popular, easily handled substitute among pastry chefs. This jar with its fastening lid ensured the sticky sweet treacle stayed where it was intended, safe from accidental spills and sticky fingers alike.[19] The treakle jar measures 6 1/2" high. *Courtesy of Joseph Nigro & Ralph Wick, Old Things Made New Again.*

Three mustard pots and a pepper pot. Left: NING PO pattern, left center: FORGET-ME-NOT, right center & far right: unidentified patterns. The pepper pot measures 4 1/2" high. *Courtesy of Joseph Nigro & Ralph Wick, Old Things Made New Again.*

NAPIER pattern ginger jar by J. & G. Alcock, dating from 1839-1846. 4" high. *Courtesy of Joseph Nigro & Ralph Wick, Old Things Made New Again.*

To keep the tea freash, SCINDE pattern tea caddy with a pewter lid, 5" high. *Courtesy of Joseph Nigro & Ralph Wick, Old Things Made New Again.*

Another ritual well established by 1800 was the tea ceremony. While tea had originally been a luxury item, by the middle of the eighteenth century it was gradually becoming a common beverage. By 1800 at least half of all American households had the teapot. For the first four decades of the nineteenth century, tea drinking among Americans increased steadily. Examples of sophisticated tea services have survived in Flow Blue from this period, testifying to the love of social tea drinking.[21]

Well established by 1800, the tea ceremony was a popular ritual with it's own rules and wares. Examples of sophisticated tea services have survived in Flow Blue from this period, testifying to the popularity of social tea drinking. AMOY sugar bowl, creamer, waste bowl, cup and saucer, and teapot by Davenport, circa 1844. *Courtesy of Joseph Nigro & Ralph Wick, Old Things Made New Again.*

AMOY tea cup and saucer and sugar bowl by Davenport. The cup measures 3 1/2" in diameter x 2 3/4" high, the saucer 6" in diameter, and the sugar bowl measures 7 1/2" high. Prior to 1860 and the introduction of granulated sugar, sugar bowls were large to accomodate portions of a broken sugar loaf. *Courtesy of Anne & Dave Middleton, Pot O' Gold Antiques.*

Habits were changing, however, by mid-century. Tea was replaced by a more powerful stimulant with a stronger flavor, coffee. During the American Civil War (1861-1865) coffee was known to be the preferred drink of both Union and Confederate armies. Union soldiers ground the beans with their rifle butts, drank four strong pints a day, and, when no fire was available, they chewed the grounds. Confederates often substituted peanuts, chicory, and even potatoes for the much desired coffee bean.[22]

Other changes occurred as well. What Charles Dickens noted about New York high society in 1842 would hold true for the growing middle class after 1850. Dickens observed, "The houses and tables are elegant; ... and there is, perhaps, a greater spirit of contention in reference to appearances, and the display of wealth and costly living." Flow Blue and other ceramic forms less expensive than porcelain but with an impressive appearance were to become major tools of the middle class in their attempts at upward mobility.[23]

PEKIN pattern coffee cup with an unidentified Wenport back mark. 4 3/8" in diameter, 3 1/8" high. *Courtesy of Joseph Nigro & Ralph Wick, Old Things Made New Again.*

By the middle of the nineteenth century, social habits were changing and coffee (a more powerful stimulant with a stronger flavor than tea) was replacing tea. A very large coffee pot in the TONQUIN pattern by Joseph Heath, dating from circa 1845 was a little ahead of the curve. 13 1/2" high. *Courtesy of Dorothy & Elmer Caskey, Trojan Antiques, Cynthiana, Kentucky 41031.*

## The Mid-Century Rise of the Middle Class

The second half of the nineteenth century saw American life continuing to change. New opportunities opened for increased income across a broader spectrum of society. New manufacturing methods produced more goods at lower prices, and rapidly expanding transportation systems allowed those products to reach more consumers than ever before. There was also, however, an increasing disparity of incomes within the populace as a whole, expanding the class consciousness of American society; a society which came to view elaborate, ritualized behaviour as a sign of sophistication. This would be expressed in many ways through all the public rituals of Victorian life. Furnishing the home, calling and visiting, and serving and conducting meals all were seen as expressions of sophistication and position in society. Flow Blue would play a role in this increasingly complex social order.[24]

Whereas during the first half of the nineteenth century, families had moved out of rural America and into cities to take advantage of new job opportunities, during the second half of the century, those who had succeeded were moving to rapidly developing suburbs. Home plans now provided ample space for public entertaining with parlors, sitting rooms, and separate dining rooms. Dining rooms had previously been absent from many house plans.[25]

These homes were filled as never before with furnishings and equipment made possible through mass production. Here manufacturers provided many Flow Blue accessories including umbrella stands, desk sets, garden seats, and jardinieres which would provide a sense of luxury in a home without overtaxing the bank account.

To provide the home and it's sur-roundings with a sense of luxury without straining the budget, Flow Blue accessories including umbrella and cane stands, desk sets, garden seats, and jardinieres were pro-duced. An umbrella and cane stand in an unidentified pattern, circa 1850. The Victorian gentleman did not consider himself to be properly dressed unless he he had his cane. The stand measures 20" high. *Cour-tesy of Dorothy & Elmer Caskey, Trojan Antiques, Cynthiana, Ken-tucky 41031.*

An ink well in Flow Blue for the desk as well, measuring 2 1/4" high, 7 1/4" wide, and 5" in di-ameter. The wells measure 2 1/2" diameter *Courtesy of Louise and Charles Loehr, Louise's Old Things, Kutztown, Pennsylvania.*

VICTORIA pattern desk set pro-duced in Austria, includes one four blotter holder, one calling card holder, a letter holder, stamp box, ink blotter, and accessories tray (for rubber bands, etc.). *Courtesy of Dorothy & Elmer Caskey, Trojan Antiques, Cynthiana, Kentucky 41031.*

A garden seat in an unidentified pattern dating from circa 1850-1860. The seat measures 18 1/2" high. *Courtesy of Dorothy & Elmer Caskey, Trojan Antiques, Cynthiana, Kentucky 41031.*

A similar garden seat from the same period. 18 1/2" high, 44 1/2" in circumference. *Courtesy of Lucille and Norman Bagdon.*

With an impressive jardiniere, the Victorian household needed an impressive jardiniere stand to display it well. Unidentified pattern produced by the Wheeling Pottery Company, an American firm. 16" high, 12 1/2" in diameter. *Courtesy of Joseph Nigro & Ralph Wick, Old Things Made New Again.*

Another impressive piece around the house was this potpourri jar, in an unidentified Flow Blue pattern. The inner lid is removed to release the potpourri's fragrant scent through the pierced outer lid. This jar measures 16" high. *Courtesy of Dorothy & Elmer Caskey, Trojan Antiques, Cynthiana, Kentucky 41031.*

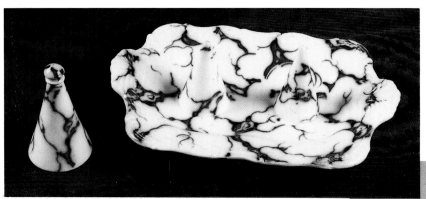

Viturally no ceramic was too small for Flow Blue as this NAVY MARBLE candle snuffer set proves. Once the snuffer has extinguished the flame, it is returned to the conical rests on the tray. *Courtesy of Dorothy & Elmer Caskey, Trojan Antiques, Cynthiana, Kentucky 41031.*

The private rooms of the Victorian home were graced with Flow Blue wares as well. Seven piece dresser set with tray in the DORIS pattern by Samuel Hancock & Sons. The set includes a hair receiver, pin trays, powder box, and candle sticks. *Courtesy of Dorothy & Arnold Kowalsky.*

Flow Blue dresser set in an unidentified rose pattern. Tray 12 1/2" x 8 1/4"; candlesticks, 6 1/4" high; flower holder 5" high; covered box 4 1/2" square and 2 1/4" high. *Courtesy of Anne & Dave Middleton, Pot O' Gold Antiques.*

An elaborate system developed for screening potential callers by recognised members of "high society" and for displaying any positive responses from the sought after individuals involving calling cards. Prior to use, the cards embossed with the name of the presentor, could rest in a calling card holder like this one in an unidentified Flow Blue pattern. It was produced by the Reinhold Schlegelmilch Porcelain Factories of Tillowitz, Silesia, Germany and dates from circa 1898-1908. 5" high. *Courtesy of Lucille and Norman Bagdon.*

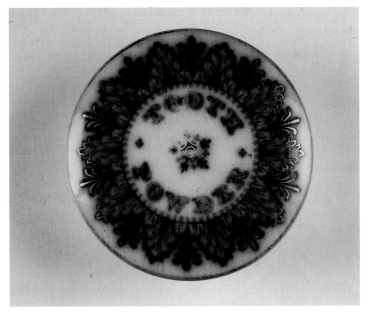

The purpose of this Flow Blue container is obvious. This tooth powder holder measures 4" in diameter and 1 3/8" in height. It is impressed 1 1/2 on the back. *Courtesy of Dorothy & Arnold Kowalsky.*

Once the house was successfully furnished, the job was to get people who could further the family's rise in society into the home and impress them. To do this, communication with recognised members of "high society" was necessary. Many families struggled to reach whomever was perceived as important. An elaborate system developed for screening potential callers and for displaying any positive responses from the sought-after individuals if they were not present themselves. This ritualized communication was based on calling cards.[26]

Calling cards were embossed with the name of the individual presenting the card. A wife carried her own and cards with her husband's name as well. During the day, a lady left home with calling cards, her carriage and a footman. The lady delivered her cards to households she wished to be associated with; the lady of that house was then obliged to at least return a card of her own to whomever had left one with her. This card could then be placed in a prominent public location in the front hall or on the mantle on a calling card plate to impress visitors with evidence of the social circles in which the family moved. Sometimes a calling card led to a personal visit from the desired personage. Occasionally this offered the opportunity to host a formal dinner party at which members of high society would be present, hopefully increasing the good fortune of the family throwing the party.[27]

## Fine Dining

The complexity and rituals permeating every aspect of Victorian life were understood to be hallmarks of mid-century civilization. Victorian food consumption was no exception, evolving into a complex, social ritual. New and developing forms of cold storage and broad transportation and delivery services allowed mid-century and later families to procure an abundance and variety of foods and to keep them from spoiling long enough to provide multi-course meals few could have matched in earlier decades. This advantage allowed for the development of the formal dinner party —at the pinnacle of nineteenth century ettiquette-bound culinary evolution.[28]

The dinner party was also recognized as one of the most reliable methods of drawing and impressing a crowd. This endeavor was not undertaken lightly. Massive tomes were written prescribing every detail from the times to serve, clothes to wear, and procedures to follow for serving ... and eating, to the very atmosphere of the dining room and who spoke to and sat next to whom. The dinner wares on which to properly serve the food also took up many pages.[29]

Here Flow Blue played a significant role as a durable ware in a variety of forms offered at prices well within the range of the aspiring middle class. By 1850 ettiquette required large matching services with a number of functionally specific pieces. Flow Blue was produced with the color, the style and the diversity of form recommended.

Extremely important to a successful dinner party was an impressive service for proper meal presentation. All the ettiquette books said so. Appearance was paramount during these multi-course extravaganzas and Flow Blue allowed the aspiring family to present the appearance of elegance without the expense. Sèvres porcelain from France would cost roughly $500 for a service. Fine Oriental services cost at least $300. Decorated English or French earthenwares with the same white colored bodies and a host of rich decorations were available from between $70 and $125 a service. In 1855 price lists show Flow Blue was still the highest priced of the transfer printed wares, but compared to Sèvres porcelain it was a bargain. As such, during the 1850s Flow Blue and other blue-and-white English earthenwares were much more commonly found gracing middle class tables than either porcelain or china.[30]

During the course of the meal, Flow Blue wares would have been employed to serve up the main courses for the middle class families seeking to impress but unable or unwilling to spring for French porcelains. For a group of twelve, the courses for the dinner party could well run to ten courses before dessert, coffee and walnuts. In the absence of the preferred French porcelains, Flow Blue would be used for the soup, game and main courses. A Chinese motif for the main course was best.[31]

The dinner party was recognized as one of the most reliable methods of drawing and impressing a crowd. By 1850 this endeavor was not undertaken lightly. Ettiquette required large matching services with a number of functionally specific peices. The aspiring middle class found Flow Blue an extremely appealing alternative to French porcelain. Flow Blue was durable, could be elegant in appearance and was always far more reasonably priced than porcelain. Flow Blue wares would have been employed to serve up the main courses for the middle class. SCINDE platter by Thomas Walker, Lion Works, Tunstall (1845-1851). The platter measures 11" x 8 3/4". *Courtesy of Anne & Dave Middleton, Pot O' Gold Antiques.*

Game and roast saddle of mutton would arrive on platters such as this PERSIANA pattern well and tree platter. It was manufactured by G. L. Ashworth, circa 1862. 19" x 15 3/8" x 2 1/4". *Courtesy of Louise and Charles Loehr, Louise's Old Things, Kutztown, Pennsylvania.*

CHUSAN chop plate by Wedgwood. *Courtesy of Dorothy & Arnold Kowalsky.*

A delicate soup was to be served. This CHUSAN pattern soup tureen by Wedgwood would have served well. It could be purchased with gold trim and without. Handle to handle, the tureen measures 13 1/2" x 11 1/2"; it is 12" high. *Courtesy of Dorothy & Arnold Kowalsky.*

CHUSAN undertray. All Wedgwood may be found with or without gold trim. 14 1/2" x 13 1/4". *Courtesy of Dorothy & Arnold Kowalsky.*

Even soup ladles were expected to reinforce the proper impression of elegance. Rare polychrome soup ladle with a JFG monogram in the center. *Courtesy of Dorothy & Arnold Kowalsky.*

Group of five sauce ladles in unidentified Flow Blue patterns. *Courtesy of Dorothy & Arnold Kowalsky.*

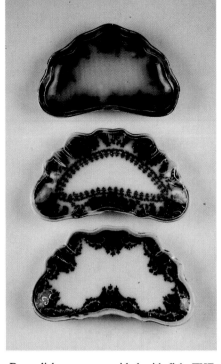

Bone dishes were provided with fish. THE BLUE DANUBE(bottom) by and FLORIDA (middle) were produced by Johnson Brothers, while AYR (top) was manufactured by W. & E. Corn. *Courtesy of Dorothy & Arnold Kowalsky.*

W. & E. Corn, Top Bridge Works, Longport (1864-1904) manufacturers' mark used from c. 1900-1904. *Courtesy of Dorothy & Arnold Kowalsky.*

A hard working hostess would be devastated if her guests overlooked the trouble she took to procure sardines, an acknowledged delicacy of the day; dishes like these were intended to make certain the guests noticed.[32] The dish also hid the tin sardines were packed in. CHUSAN sardine dishes by Wedgwood with an octagonal cut. The undertray measures 6 5/8" x 5 1/2". The box 4 5/8" x 3 3/8" x 3 3/4" high. *Courtesy of Dorothy & Arnold Kowalsky.*

Major pieces came and went from the table with each successive course, laden with soups, turtles, fish, lobsters, venison, roast saddle of mutton or stewed beef à la jardinière, a plethora of vegetable, side dishes, wines, and desserts to delight even the most rosy-cheeked, overstuffed, walrus mustachioed Victorian man. The impact of the parading dinner wares themselves were transitory however. Small ceramic wares littered the table and were not removed. These helped enforce a positive lasting impression. To this end a wide variety of butter pats, individual salts, table salts, sugar bowls, and cream and syrup pitchers were produced in Flow Blue.[33]

Small ceramic wares remained on the table while plates, platters and tureens came and went, reinforcing a positive lasting impression of the elegance of the dinner. CHUSAN pattern pepper pots, master salts, and mustards by Wedgwood. This is a unique set. Peppers, 5", mustards 4", and salts 2" high. *Courtesy of Dorothy & Arnold Kowalsky.*

Butter pats, read top to bottom, left to right, patterns: OXFORD, FLORIDA, MELBOURNE, RICHMOND (Johnson Brothers), ROSEVILLE (Maddock & Son), JANETTE (W.H. Grindley), DERBY (W.H. Grindley), and two unidentified Oriental scenes. All average 3" to 3 1/4" in diameter. *Courtesy of Dorothy & Arnold Kowalsky.*

Two condiment sets with mustard, salt dip and pepper in silver stands. Perfect accents to the flowing table. *Courtesy of Lucille and Norman Bagdon.*

A variety of cups with a variety of purposes for varying occasions. Left to right: COBURG punch cup, SHANGHAE punch cup by J. Furnival, MANILLA posset cup, LOZERN punch cup, FORMOSA chocolate cup, and TONQUIN chocolate cup. Measurements vary from 2 1/4" in diameter and 2 1/2" high to 3" in diameter and 3 3/4" high. *Courtesy of Joseph Nigro & Ralph Wick, Old Things Made New Again.*

Dessert services were designed to finish an impressive dinner party with a flourish. This CHUSAN pattern dessert service includes two nut dishes, two tazzas with single tab handles, two cake plates with four tabs, a pedestalled cake plate and pedestalled fruit dish. This particular sercive did not come to the America, however. It went to Scotland. Nut dishes: 6 1/4" x 4 1/2", 2 tazzas with single tab handles: 9" to tab x 8 1/2", pedestalled cake stand: 11 1/4" x 2 1/4" high, 2 cake plates with 4 tabs: 11" x 8 1/2", pedestalled fruit: 10 1/8" x 7 1/2" x 3" high. *Courtesy of Dorothy & Arnold Kowalsky.*

Dessert services were designed to finish that impressive dinner party with a flourish. The service itself, lavishly decorated with tasteful flowers and fruits and made of the most expensive material a family could afford, consisted generally of compotes with varying heights, at least two cake plates and twelve dessert plates. Once again the display was as important as the bright fruits, cakes, and candies served.[34]

ALMA pattern tazza, no manufacturer identified. 12" x 2 3/4". *Courtesy of Joseph Nigro & Ralph Wick, Old Things Made New Again.*

Reticulated, pedestalled cake stand with an unidentified pattern. This is considered to be scarce with reticulation. Height 3 1/2", 9" diameter *Courtesy of Dorothy & Arnold Kowalsky.*

During the second half of the nineteenth century a fascination with hothouse plants created a secondary craze for strawberries, preferably home grown.[35] STRAWBERRY brushstroke pattern, unidentified maker, two teapots and one pitcher. The pitcher measures 7" to the spout; the teapots measure 10 3/4" and 9 3/4" high. *Courtesy of Joseph Nigro & Ralph Wick, Old Things Made New Again.*

STRAWBERRY mulberry platter, octagonal with double scalloped corners. This pattern comes in Flow Blue and polychrome as well and is considered scarce. 11 1/4" x 9 3/4". *Courtesy of Dorothy & Arnold Kowalsky.*

After the last dish was served and dinner drew to a close, the ladies withdrew and gentlemen passed the port, smoked, and spoke freely. This continued until the host decided the port and conversation was flowing a little too freely. Then the gentlemen were returned to their ladies and to civility. This SCINDE tobacco-jar by Samuel Alcock would be just the thing for storing tobacco for such an occasion. The jar measures 5 3/4" in diameter and 9" high. *Courtesy of Joseph Nigro & Ralph Wick, Old Things Made New Again.*

Eventually, food laden dishes stopped coming and the formal dinner drew to a close. Ladies withdrew to the drawing room upstairs for coffee or tea. Gentlemen then passed the port. As a gentleman never smoked the the presence of a lady, this was the time when men so inclined would indulge. Cigars were preferred as these were considered symbols of status and manly wealth. Smoking wares in Flow Blue were produced to accommodate this need as well. Only when the port and speech began to flow too freely would the host suggest the gentlemen return to their ladies and wind down the evening.[36]

Breakfast, tea and dessert also required their own special wares. During the first half of the nineteenth century breakfast sets had consisted of twelve cups and saucers with larger teacups than would generally be used for other occasions, a sugar dish, a milk pot, teapot, slop bowl and breakfast plates. Larger sets would include a coffee pot, butter boat, and cake plate. By the end of the nineteenth century, breakfast included fruit and a mush -hot cereal of boiled grains. These required a fruit plate and mush bowl.[37]

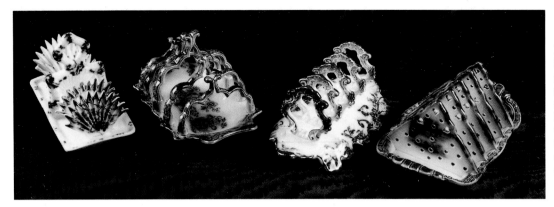

Breakfast tables may also have included toast holders, which in my experience are perfectly designed to leave breakfasters with cold toast in seconds. Four toast holders in unidentified patterns without manufacturers' marks. *Courtesy of Dorothy & Elmer Caskey, Trojan Antiques, Cynthiana, Kentucky 41031.*

Breakfast required special wares all it's own. By the end of the nineteenth century, among these were mush cups. MADRAS pattern, large breakfast mush cup or "farmers cup." The cup measures 4 1/4" high and 4 5/8" along it's inside diameter. *Courtesy of Dorothy & Arnold Kowalsky.*

Afternoon tea began in the 1840s in England and soon extended to America. Tea services for five o'clock tea, a ritual in-and-of itself by the 1860s, were comprised of a teapot, sugar bowl, creamer, cups and saucers, cup plates, a waste bowl, plates, two cake plates, preserve plates, a butter plate, a tray, hot-water urn, spoon holder, and occasionally a syrup or molasses pitcher. Breakfasts and teas could be served on a rotating table in the budoir as well. With Flow Blue on the table reducing cost, who knows, maybe a higher quality cup of tea could be served.[38]

ARABESQUE sugar bowl manufactured by T. J. & J. Mayer as well but with another pattern design. 7 1/2" high. *Courtesy of Anne & Dave Middleton, Pot O' Gold Antiques.*

The tea ritual was considered highly important and special attire for the event existed by the 1870s. The Ladys Companion, an 1851 manual for proper living and hostessing presented a harrowing tale of an unthinking husband who brought important newly married guests home unannounced at tea time. The poor hostess was having a simple tea with her nephew. Not anticipating any guests of social stature, she was using only the black kettle and Rockingham teapot, rather than the urn and a better service. This particular tea was to be a cozy, private affair set on the small tea table by the fire. Then husband and guests arrived unexpectedly. So shocked by this untimely arrival was the hostess, she leapt to her feet, upsetting the table. The dishevelled hostess was then introduced to her guests and the unfortunate social gaff was descirbed as follows, "The lady bowed coldly, as if she felt that she was an elegant woman, and an excellent match — and now behold us! My cheeks flushed, my hair untidy, no milk, and the elegant bride by my side, ..."[39]

Five o'clock afternoon teas began in England in the 1840s and soon spread to America. These occasions required their own special services as well. ARABESQUE pattern teapot manufactured by Thomas, John & Joseph Mayer, circa 1851. 8 1/2" high. *Courtesy of Louise and Charles Loehr, Louise's Old Things, Kutztown, Pennsylvania.*

Fortunately the trusty maid Jane brings an appropriately formal tea service and more milk. The potentially grievous social blunder is saved, "The milk came — the tea was over, and the company safe in our drawing room." After the guests left, the troubled hostess slumped exhausted onto a small sofa and, hand on head, announced to her thoughtless spouse that if he ever put her in such social peril again she would surely die. For the Victorians, even an afternoon tea was serious business, demanding a properly elegant tea service and all due decorum.[40]

Children used Flow Blue as well. This pap boat could serve a young childs or an invalids meal. 4 3/4" long. *Courtesy of Lucille and Norman Bagdon.*

Not all Flow Blue in the latter half of the nineteenth century was produced to engage in social one-upmanship. Some simply put a smile on the face. SINGA two scene cup by Cork, Edge & Melkin, and SLOE BLOSSOM pattern mugs both have frogs in the bottom. They measure 4 1/2" dia, 3 3/4" diameter *Courtesy of Joseph Nigro & Ralph Wick, Old Things made new again.*

Children love to emulate their parents (sometimes much to our chagrin). Children's sets in Flow Blue allowed for this sometimes mutually educational play. CRINES PAGODA patterned child's wash ewer and bowl. No manufacturer is identified on the mark. The bowl measures 9 1/2" in diameter and 3 1/4" high; the pitcher measures 7 1/2" to the spout. *Courtesy of Lucille and Norman Bagdon.*

Child's partial tea set in a NAVY MARBLE pattern. This set may have been produced by Charles Meigh. *Courtesy of Dorothy & Arnold Kowalsky.*

Child's teapot in the BLUE BELL pattern by one of the several Hackwoods potting in Shelton and Hanley from 1827-1855. 4 1/2" high. *Courtesy of Dorothy & Elmer Caskey, Trojan Antiques, Cynthiana, Kentucky 41031.*

By the late nineteenth century, manufacturers had expanded their production capacities and distribution networks to provide a wider choice of wares for all occasions to every socio-economic level. Late nineteenth century Flow Blue reflects this trend with wares exhibiting a wide range of qualities produced by well known and obscure manufacturers from Britian, America and Europe. Here are some of their more unusual products: a toast holder 7 1/2" in length and 4 3/4" high, a ceramic ball 10 1/2" in circumference, and two doorknobs. *Courtesy of Dorothy & Arnold Kowalsky.*

Having washed and had their five o'clock tea, children were ready to carry out an imaginary dinner party. CHINESE BELLS child's set with a "large" tureen and underplate, gravy boat and covered vegetable. These were produced by James Edwards, circa 1845. The tureen stands 4 3/4" high. *Courtesy of Dorothy & Elmer Caskey, Trojan Antiques, Cynthiana, Kentucky 41031.*

A closer look at the underplate of the CHINESE BELLS patterned Childs set. *Courtesy of Dorothy & Elmer Caskey, Trojan Antiques, Cynthiana, Kentucky 41031.*

To accomodate the new demand for tablewares of all sorts, manufacturers expanded their production capacities and distribution networks. By the end of the nineteenth century this expansion would lead to a wide choice of services for all occasions available at every socio-economic level. Late nineteenth century Flow Blue reflects this trend with wares exhibiting a wide range of qualities produced by well known and obscure manufacturers from Britian, America and Europe.[41]

Providing the diversity of wares necessary for Victorian custom and ritual to as many people as possible, and keeping in tune with the ever changing and evolving tastes of their customers, required manufacturers to develop sophisticated means of communicating with the public and of checking on developing trends in the arts world-wide. Daunting as that task may seem, by mid-century manufacturers had found a way to accomplish both at once through government sponsored international exhibitions.

## International Exhibitions

The first grand international exhibition was inspired by that pervasive British feeling of security and prosperity. In 1849 Prince Albert and a colleague from the Royal Society of Arts, Henry Cole, began planning for the first international exhibition in England. The basic idea was to compare British industry with that of the rest of the "civilized" world. Britian was to come out ahead in the comparison, of course. The Great Exhibition of the Industry of All Nations was hosted in London in the newly built Crystal Palace in 1851. The intended result was apparently achieved as exhibitions continued throughout the rest of the century.[42]

There were eleven major international exhibitions between 1851 and 1889:

Great Exhibiton of the Industry of All Nations, London, 1851.
Universal Exhibition, Paris, 1855.
International Exhibition, London, 1862.
Universal Exhibition, Paris, 1867.
International Exhibition, London, 1871.
Universal Exhibition, Vienna, 1873.
International Exhibition, London, 1874.
Philadelphia Centennial Exhibition, Philadelphia, 1876.
Universal Exhibition, Paris, 1878.
International Exhibition, Sydney, 1880.
Universal Exhibition, Paris, 1889.[43]

international exhibitions played a pivotal role in the further development of first British, then European and finally American ceramics manufacture, style and consumption. A number of manufacturers attended them all. The benefits for competitive manufacturers were three-fold.

First, manufacturers from all over the globe displayed a tremendous range of wares. Clever exhibitors spent time touring competitors exhibits, collecting traditional manufacturing and stylistic techniques never before seen in the host country. New developments were widely and rapidly disseminated as never before.

Second, wares were judged and awards presented at each exhibition. The competition to present new and improved wares at each exhibit was intense. Investments in research and development were made and the best designers, modellers and decorators were hired. Wares were quickly improved to garner the favor of judges and the prestiege a winning medal could provide. Some manufacturers created exclusive and extravagant touring stock solely for these events.

Third, these international exhibitions drew huge crowds.

Over six million visitors attended the Great Exhibition of 1851. No better forum to present a manufacturer's wares to the public or to create new demand for them existed at this time. Demand was created and stylistic trends were set at these exhibitions. Exotic wares from foreign lands often made their first appearance at these events.[44]

The popularity of international exhibitions among competing manufacturers is evident in the total numbers of exhibitors present or in the numbers of prizes awarded. The Paris Exhibition of 1867 featured 43,237 exhibitors; the Universal Exhibition in Paris in 1878 presented 22,100 awards. Competition was fierce among ceramics manufacturers. The opportunity to improve their standing, their products and their visibility with the buying public was just too good for manufacturers to pass up.[45]

The 1851 Great Exhibition had a dramatic positive effect on British industry. Flow Blue manufacturers were present among the many exhibitors as noted in the Reports by the Juries on the Subject in the Thirty Classes into Which the Exhibition Was Divided, sent to American officials in 1852. This report explained the juries' results. Listed among the exhibiting Staffordshire potters were T. Dimmock, C. Mason, T.J. & J. Mayer, Minton, J. Ridgway & Company, and Wedgwood & Son. The jury took particular note of Dimmock's Flow Blue, stating, "This manufacturer has exhibited ... earthenware of first-rate quality, and the Jury have much admired the neatness and good taste of his printed patterns, *the agreeable effect of his 'flowing blue,'* and the general excellence of his ware."[46]

For international exhibitions, some manufacturers created exclusive and extravagant touring stock which could be complex in execution or extraordinarily large to catch the eye of both the public and the judges. KYBER teapot by W. Adams & Co. and KYBER coffee pot by John Meir & Son. The coffee pot is unusually large, measuring 11 1/4" high. The teapot is more standard, measuring 7 1/4" high. *Courtesy of Louise and Charles Loehr, Louise's Old Things, Kutztown, Pennsylvania.*

John Meir & Son, Greengates Pottery, Tunstall, manufacturers' mark and KYBER pattern name from coffeepot. This printed J. M. & S. mark dates from 1837-1897. *Courtesy of Louise and Charles Loehr, Louise's Old Things, Kutztown, Pennsylvania.*

Thomas Dimmock caught the eye of the judges at the International Exhibition at the Crystal Palace in London in 1851. They made approving comments about the effect of his "flowing blue." BAMBOO pattern creamer by Thomas Dimmock. *Courtesy of Dorothy & Arnold Kowalsky.*

A brief note was also made of the American presence among the ceramicists in 1851, "One article is shown from America." The jury was apparently unimpressed. There is no mention of any award received. For that matter, there is not even a mention of the American manufacturers *name*.[47]

Failure to make a positive impression with the 1851 jury was symptomatic of a greater problem American potters faced at home. They could not shake the long held belief in the superiority of their English counterparts wares. They saw an opportunity to change that perception at the 1876 Philadelphia Centennial Exhibition and seized it.

In 1875 the first National Association of Potters was formed in Philadelphia with representatives of 70 factories present from around the nation. Most were from established potting centers in Trenton, New Jersey and East Liverpool, Ohio. At the meeting they resolved that there was sufficient talent in America to create new designs which were more elegant and suitable to Americans. Foreign patterns were not to be copied.[48]

Part of this confidence in the face of consumer obstinance surely stemmed from the high duties placed on imported ceramics in 1861 by the United States Congress. As a result, British potters had opened factories within the nations' borders to avoid the duties. No doubt this was calculated as part of that "sufficient talent."[49]

The results of the National Association's resolve were displayed at the Centennial Exhibition the following year. A positive impression was necessary at the massive affair. The Centennial Exhibition sprawled across 60 acres and featured five main exhibition halls and 155 other structures. There would be no better chance to prove American ability to a larger crowd than this.[50]

The importance of the exhibition for American potters can not be overstated. The public was looking for diversions from the litany of political scandals, financial and mercantile collapses and working-class discontent. The fair's backers were looking to restore public confidence in the strength of American enterprise. Potters were looking to create confidence in the quality of American wares. On opening day, May 10, 1876, 186,672 visitors passed through the halls. By the Exhibitions close in mid-November nearly 10 million — almost one fifth of the total population of the United States at that time had been exposed to the wares on display.[51]

The handicraft of many nations was there. The English pottery firm Brown-Westhead, Moore & Company of Staffordshire was one of the American potters' old rivals present for immediate comparison, testing the new resolve of American potters to best the British at their own game. New techniques and styles were quickly acquired. The Pavillion of the Empire of Japan was of particular interest to the audience and exhibitors. Of the building itself, the Centennial Exposition Guide raved, "This building...causes astonishment at its beauty and elegance of finish. It is regarded as the finest piece of carpenter-work in this country..." Despite negative feelings for Japan and other foreign powers in the crowd as indicated by the remainder of the Guide's review, "Some of our more progressive mechanics were inclined to ridicule the leisurely manner in which the Japanese workmen labored, ..." manufacturers and the public alike were impressed, "...but they find that if the work was done slowly, it was done remarkably well." In the years that followed, despite an undercurrent of prejudice, great quantities of American Flow Blue produced after the Centennial exhibited Japanese influence.[52]

The 1876 exhibition's effect on American industry was as dramatic as the 1851 exhibition's had been on English manufacturers a quarter century earlier. Edwin Barber, a noted nineteenth century ceramics historian, later remarked, "The existance of a true ceramic art in this country may be said to have commenced with the fair of 1876, greater progress has been made within the last fifteen years which have elapsed since that important event than during the two centuries which preceded it." During the last quarter of the nineteenth a number of American potteries successfully produced and marketed Flow Blue.[53]

After a long struggle and bouyed by success at the Centennial Exhibition in Philadelphia, American potteries successfully produced and marketed Flow Blue. "La Belle" chocolate pot and cups by the Wheeling Pottery Company of Wheeling, West Virginia. The pot measures 7 1/2" to the spout, the saucers measure 5" in diameter, and the cups measure 2 1/2" in diameter and 3 1/4" high. *Courtesy of Joseph Nigro & Ralph Wick, Old Things Made New Again.*

## Inspirations and Movements

Artisitic movements, discoveries of exotic foreign traditions, and an increasing sophistication in the public's taste changed the face of Flow Blue throughout the nineteenth century. Each successive movement and discovery provided impetus and inspiration for innovation in transfer printed designs and vessel forms. Among the movements and discoveries were an early taste for Chinoiseries, Romanticism, a growing interest in natural history, the discovery of Japanisme, the Aesthetic Movement, the Arts and Crafts movement, and in the waning years of the nineteenth century, Art Nouveau.

## Chinoiserie and the Romantic Movement

The earliest designs were predominantly Oriental motifs, Chinioseries, building on the popularity of Chinese export porcelain. The popularity of British and American historical views from early in the century led to the creation of scenic designs in early Flow Blue which were also heavily influenced by the Romantic movement.[54]

The earliest designs were predominantly Oriental motifs. CHINESE LANDSCAPE by G. L. Ashworth using the Mason's Patent Ironstone China manufacturers' mark, circa 1862. 10 1/4" in diameter. *Courtesy of Dorothy & Elmer Caskey, Trojan Antiques, Cynthiana, Kentucky 41031.*

Chinoiseries built on the popularity of Chinese export porcelain. CABUL charger or chop plate by James Edwards, dating to 1847. 11" in diameter. *Courtesy of Joseph Nigro & Ralph Wick, Old Things Made New Again.*

The Romantic movement of the first half of the nineteenth century effected the landscapes, both domestic and oriental. The views were romanticised, idealized portrayals of places or events. Even country scenes were enhanced with sentimental devices. The romantic view either looked longingly back to the pre-Industrial age or towards the wonders of nature and their meaning. Three subjects were considered most attractive in these views: scenes from literature and mythology, subjects of common human experience, and nostaligic, exotic, sublime or historical subjects. All were designed to produced predictable, preconditioned responses in all viewers. To create oriental views which would elicit the appropriate response, a wide range of oriental elements were swirled together to create pleasing, eye-catching designs.[55]

One of the three subjects considered most attractive in the romantic view was a scene from literature or mythology. Small vase featuring mythological characters in an unidentified pattern. There is no manufacturers' mark. 5 1/4" high. *Courtesy of Joseph Nigro & Ralph Wick, Old Things Made New Again.*

The mythological romantic view at work again. Bread Plate in an unidentified design. Once again there were no marks. 11" in diameter. *Courtesy of Louise and Charles Loehr, Louise's Old Things, Kutztown, Pennsylvania.*

The second of the three subjects involved material of common human experience. Two molded pitchers featuring two boys playing cards amidst idle cleaning supplies, a very common shared experience. 8" high to the spout and 5 3/4" high to the spout. *Courtesy of Louise and Charles Loehr, Louise's Old Things, Kutztown, Pennsylvania.*

Nature's landscapes were imbued with moral as well as emotional impact. Groves of trees created no mere forests, they were God's first temples. The messages carried within the motifs were expected to be readable by all. Dinner was to be an educational and uplifting affair.[56]

In a bizarre twist on Romanticism, death was romanticized early in the nineteenth century. This would lead to a rising interest in Egyptian art and death symbology in the United States. The end of the common man's life was seen as sweet melancholy. The Garden Cemetery Movement arose from this view to create the first major American cemetery, Mount Auburn, in Boston, Massachusetts in 1831. The 72 acre burial ground was considered a beautiful open space for picnics and public education. The Movement also created an appreciation for sculpture, particularly sculpture with an Egyptian theme as Egyptian symbology, mysterious and imposing, was the symbology of the dead.[57] SPHINX pattern sauce tureen and underplate by Charles Meigh, circa 1840. 6" high, underplate 8 1/2" x 7 3/4". *Courtesy of Lucille and Norman Bagdon.*

## Natural History

As improved transportation systems allowed Victorians to more conveniently and extensively explore the world, a passion for natural history developed. This passion had them chronicling what they were not consuming of the planet's flora, fauna and sea life, creating museums for their discoveries, erecting home conservatories and publishing illustrated volumes on the natural sciences. It sent Flow Blue artisans thumbing through botany texts, and visiting botanical gardens and zoos, sketch pads in hand, for inspiration.[58]

Victorian artisans were busy documenting the planet's flora, fauna and sea life as intrepid explorers pushed onward. SHELL potato bowl reflects the Victorian passion for the growing study of conchology. This potato bowl was manufactured by Edward Challinor (1842-1867) and measures 10" in diameter. *Courtesy of Joseph Nigro & Ralph Wick, Old Things Made New Again.*

Victorians became fascinated with the natural world as they pushed on in their explorations, aided by the technologies of the industrial revolution. They chronicled whatever they encountered. *Courtesy of the author's collection.*

Following the international exhibitions of 1862 and 1867, Japanese designs caught the English popular imagination as Chinese export porcelain had a century before. Fans and cherry blossom motifs soon appeared in Flow Blue. Unidentified shallow bowl with Japanese fan and cherry blossom motif by Mintons, 1877. 10 3/8" in diameter and 1 1/2" high. *Courtesy of Louise and Charles Loehr, Louise's Old Things, Kutztown, Pennsylvania.*

The passion for nature sent Flow Blue artisans searching through botany texts, botanical gardens and zoos for inspiration. GERANEUM pattern sugar bowl, Podmore, Walker & Company (1834-1859). 7 1/2" high. *Courtesy of Dorothy & Elmer Caskey, Trojan Antiques, Cynthiana, Kentucky 41031.*

## Japanese

Japanese motifs entered into English Flow Blue designs after the South Kensington Exhibition of 1862 and the Paris Exhibition of 1867. They appeared in American design following the 1876 Centennial Exhibition in Philadelphia. Japanese designs caught the English popular imagination as Chinese export porcelian had a century before. Ornate ornamentation fell away in the face of a new appreciation for Japanese design elements based on simplicity, symmetry of form and ornament, and use of less continuous decoration. The enthusaism for Japanese art also displayed itself in fan and cherry blossom motifs. By the mid-1870s Japanaese decorative ideas were incorporated into the Aesthetic Movement.[59]

## The Aesthetic and the Arts and Crafts Movements

While the Industrial Revolution brought lower prices and social change to the Western world, it also marred the landscape with industrial wastes. The Art Journal Illustrated Catalog of 1851 provided an insight into the intensity of the problem in their review of Charles Meigh and Sons establishment. According to the catalog, the factory was one of the largest and oldest in the Staffordshire district, consuming 250 tons of coal and 80 tons of clay every week. The coal smoke from that one factory alone must have created formidable problems.[60]

The Aesthetic Movement was a social and artistic reaction to the ugliness that was a by-product of the industrial age. It favored simplicity of design over past complexity which suited both the naturalistic and stylized designs employed in England by 1870. While its emblems, the sunflower and peacock, played no significant role in Flow Blue, the idea of simplified form and stylized nature was applied.[61]

During the last quarter of the nineteenth century, Arts and Crafts styles came into favor, characterized by curved designs taken from the natural shapes of flowers and plants. Gone were fancy embellishments and excessive decorative techniques. They were no longer associated with skillful work in the publics mind. This was highly stylized nature, graced with a simplicity of design. Japanese art was influential during this period as well.[62]

## Art Nouveau

The final years of Flow Blue production overlapped the Art Nouveau movement rising at the end of the nineteenth century. Considered to be a return to nature, Art Nouveau was a fusion of Japanese naturalism and French and Italian Renaissance scrolled and foliate ornament. Designs were intended to be gracefully fluid, a stylized evolution of natural art motifs. W. B. Honey, the keeper of the Department of Ceramics at the Victoria and Albert Museum, wrote of the Art Nouveau style in 1933, "In England the movement chiefly resulted in a school-taught curliness ...".[63]

The final years of Flow Blue production overlapped the Art Nouveau movement rising at the end of the nineteenth century. BURLEIGH soup tureen by Burgess & Leigh, circa 1903. 6 1/2" high. *Courtesy of Anne & Dave Middleton, Pot O' Gold Antiques.*

Art Nouveau was a fusion of Japanese naturalism and French and Italian Renaissance scrolled and foliate ornament. Unidentified patten pedestalled vase with a registry number (5314899) indicating a date between 1905 and 1909. 7" high. *Courtesy of Joseph Nigro & Ralph Wick, Old Things Made New Again.*

# Chapter 3.
# A Survey of British, American and European Flow Blue Manufacturers

This chapter surveys a number of the influential firms producing Flow Blue from its introduction through the early twentieth century. For convenience, the chapter is divided into three sections by country or continent of origins. Within each section the potteries are listed in alphabetical order. With the potteries are also added some of the patterns each pottery produced. Given the enormous number of patterns produced throughout the nineteenth century, this listing of patterns will not even pretend to be complete. Also, as a matter of expediency, a single endnote citation will cover each potter, thus limiting the number of endnote designations necessary in this section.

## British Manufacturers

The Staffordshire Pottery district was a major center of British ceramics manufacturing. By the Great International Exhibition of the Works of All Nations in 1851, Staffordshire was home to 133 factories, fully two-thirds of the British pottery industry. By 1880 over 50,000 individuals were employed by or dependent on the Staffordshire potteries. The main "Pottery Towns" comprising the district were Burslem, Cobridge, Dresden, Etruria, Fenton, Longport, Longton, Hanley, Shelton, Stoke-on-Trent, and Tunstall. Of these, Stoke-on-Trent was the rail hub.[1]

Small potteries vastly outnumbered large and well known firms. The smaller potteries followed the lead of the larger, more established firms who set the trends, taking advantage of the new demands established by their larger counterparts. Domestic tableware comprised the bulk of the output of the Staffordshire potteries.[2]

## The Adams Family

The Adams family produced a long and prodigous line of creative Staffordshire potters with an unfortunate lack of creativity in naming sons. They proclaim a 1657 date of establishment and continue to produce ceramic wares today. During the first half of the nineteenth century, three cousins named William Adams worked several Staffordshire potteries. The William Adams born in 1745, once apprenticed to Josiah Wedgwood, operated out of Greengates, Tunstall from 1779-1805. He produced a variety of earthenwares including blue jasper wares with white reliefs in the Wedgwood-style. On his death in 1805, his son Benjamin Adams ran the Tunstall operation, turning out high quality blue transfer printed pearlware impressed B. ADAMS.

KYBER Salad Bowl with stand by W. Adams and Company, circa 1891, bowl 9 1/4" in diameter and 4 3/4" high; the underplate measures 13" from handle to handle x 10 1/2". *Courtesy of Louise and Charles Loehr, Louise's Old Things, Kutztown, Pennsylvania.*

William Adams, operating the Greenfield Works of Stoke-on-Trent from 1804-1829 specialized in blue transfer printed earthenware. His offerings featured patriotic scenes, historical personages and scenic views for export to the United States. His work compared well with the Wedgwood style and quality. Adams also produced quality earthenwares enjoyed both in the home market and abroad. The Stoke-on-Trent works would pass out of the Adams family's hands in 1863.

William Adams and his sons William and Thomas, son and grandsons of William Adams of Stoke-on-Trent, operated the Greenfield Works of Tunstall. The Greenfield Works were originally established in Stoke-on-Trent by William Adams father who ran the works under his own name until 1829. In 1834 Greenfield opened new works at Tunstall with his son William at the helm. In 1865 the firm passed to his sons, William and Thomas.

The Greenfield Works concentrated on the export trade, producing wares for the United States, Central America, Brazil, Cuba, Manila, Singapore and other foreign markets. The Adams' wares from Greenfield Works consisted of tea and table services, toilet sets and other domestic wares bearing decorations Llewellynn Jewitt described in 1877 as having a "...the bright fancy character of which is much admired in the out-markets of the world ..." The William Adams and Company mark may be found on Flow Blue in Fairy Villas, Garland, Kyber, and Tedworth patterns. William Adams & Sons produced Jeddo and Tonquin patterns.

## Marks

The Adams family marks usually incorporate the family name, Adams. W. Adams & Sons used W.A. & S. or the firms full name. A variety of printed backstamps were produced, often incorporating the trade names of the pattern or the body.[3]

## Alcock

"...the finer descriptions of earthenware, one of their [Samuel Alcock's] specialities being semi-porcelain of fine and durable quality." — Llewellynn Jewitt, 1877.

Samuel Alcock produced pottery and porcelain in a wide variety of wares from Staffordshire from c. 1828-1859. Wares ranged from inexpensive domestic wares to finely crafted bone china and earthenwares. Alcock rebuilt an old Burslem pottery of Ralph Wood's in circa 1830, the Hill Pottery. His wares for domestic and foreign markets included Flow Blue in the Bamboo, Carlton, Hyson, Kremlin and Oriental patterns, Rockingham-style tablewares, molded jugs in Parian ware dating from the late 1840s, and decorative vases. While much of Samuel Alcocks work went unmark, there were distinctive shapes employed which were registered and bear a registration mark. Each registered shape was produced in several sizes and decorated in a wide variety of designs. Samuel Alcock also employed a system of fractional pattern numbers. These help to identify his wares.

ORIENTAL cake plate by Samuel Alcock & Company, 12" in diameter, 3 3/4" high. *Courtesy of Dorothy & Elmer Caskey, Trojan Antiques, Cynthiana, Kentucky 41031.*

 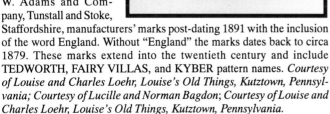

W. Adams and Company, Tunstall and Stoke, Staffordshire, manufacturers' marks post-dating 1891 with the inclusion of the word England. Without "England" the marks dates back to circa 1879. These marks extend into the twentieth century and include TEDWORTH, FAIRY VILLAS, and KYBER pattern names. *Courtesy of Louise and Charles Loehr, Louise's Old Things, Kutztown, Pennsylvania; Courtesy of Lucille and Norman Bagdon; Courtesy of Louise and Charles Loehr, Louise's Old Things, Kutztown, Pennsylvania.*

John and George Alcock were also established in Cobridge. They were producing earthenwares from 1839 to 1846. While Jewitt had nothing to say of their accomplishments, John and George Alcock produced Flow Blue in Napier and Scinde patterns. A partnership of John and Samuel Alcock, Junior succeeded John and George Alcock at Cobridge from c. 1848 to 1850.

## Marks

Samuel Alcock's marks were mainly printed. There were several including the name "S Alcock & Co." At times only the initials "S A & Co." were used.

Samuel Alcock & Company, Cobridge and Burslem, Staffordshire, printed initials manufacturers' marks used from circa 1830-1859 with BAMBOO and KREMLIN pattern names. *Courtesy of Louise and Charles Loehr, Louise's Old Things, Kutztown, Pennsylvania; Courtesy of Dorothy & Elmer Caskey, Trojan Antiques, Cynthiana, Kentucky 41031.*

John and George Alcock used impressed marks with the name "J & G ALCOCK" combined either with the "COBRIDGE" town name or with the name of the ceramic body "ORIENTAL STONE". Another ceramic body identification on their ironstone was "ALCOCKS INDIAN IRONSTONE". This firm also used the initials "J. & G. A." on several impressed or printed marks.

SCINDE undertray by J. & G. Alcock, 9 1/8" square. *Courtesy of Joseph Nigro & Ralph Wick, Old Things Made New Again.*

Henry Alcock & Company (Ltd.) was in operation from 1861 to 1910. This firm was located at the Elder Pottery in Cobridge, the successor of John Alcock (1853-1861) and the predecessor of The Henry Alcock Pottery (1910-1935). As with the other Alcock potteries, Henry Alcock & Company produced earthenwares including Flow Blue in the Delamere, Manhattan, and Touraine patterns.

J. & G. Alcock, Cobridge, Staffordshire, impressed manufacturers' name mark dating from 1839-1846. Oriental Stone refers to the body of the ware, not the pattern. *Courtesy of Anne & Dave Middleton, Pot O' Gold Antiques.*

Henry Alcock & Company produced printed marks with the initials "H. A. & Co." from 1860-1880 or with the full name of the pottery. The name of the country of origin, "ENGLAND", was added in 1891 and "Ltd." was added to the company name in 1900.[4]

DELAMERE soup ladle by Henry Alcock and Company. *Courtesy of Dorothy & Arnold Kowalsky.*

Henry Alcock & Company, Cobridge, Staffordshire, printed crown and shield mark with manufacturers' name and TOURAINE pattern name, 1891-1910. The registry number indicates a registration date of 1898. *Courtesy of Louise and Charles Loehr, Louise's Old Things, Kutztown, Pennsylvania.*

## George L. & Taylor Ashworth

This firm operated out of the Broad Street Works in Hanley, the works where Mason's Patent Ironstone China as well as the Ironstone China of the earlier firm of Hicks, Meigh, and Johnson were produced. George L and Taylor Ashworth bought the company and began operations in 1862, complete with the former company's molds, copper plates and all. They continued to produce ironstone under the name Real Ironstone China. They used the best patterns and molds Mason had devised for his services as well as Meigh's molds. The patterns Chinese Landscape, Persiana and Ruins were produced in Flow Blue by Messrs. Ashworth.

G. L. Ashworth & Bros. (Ltd.), Hanley, Staffordshire, ASHWORTH impressed manufacturers' mark used from 1862-1880. *Courtesy of Louise and Charles Loehr, Louise's Old Things, Kutztown, Pennsylvania.*

G. L. Ashworth & Bros. (Ltd.), Hanley, Staffordshire, impressed ASHWORTH REAL IRONSTONE CHINA mark in use from circa 1862-1891. *Courtesy of Dorothy & Elmer Caskey, Trojan Antiques, Cynthiana, Kentucky 41031.*

CHINESE LANDSCAPE covered vegetable by George L. & Taylor Ashworth. The Ashworth brothers made use of the Mason's Real Ironstone China manufacturers' mark. *Courtesy of Dorothy & Elmer Caskey, Trojan Antiques, Cynthiana, Kentucky 41031.*

G. L. Ashworth & Bros. (Ltd.), Hanley, Staffordshire, printed Mason's Patent Ironstone China mark in use circa 1862. They later added their own name "ASHWORTHS'" beneath the mark. *Courtesy of Dorothy & Elmer Caskey, Trojan Antiques, Cynthiana, Kentucky 41031.*

The brothers Ashworth produced table, dessert and toilet wares along with ornamental goods. They also produced vases and jugs with handles molded in the forms of dragons and other fanciful beasts. In 1877 Jewitt considered their work to be of the best quality. The company is still in business today.

### Marks

George L. and Taylor Ashworth employed several printed marks of their own with the initials or name of the firm including "A. BROS.", "G.L.A. & BROS.", "ASHWORTH BROS." and "G.L. Ashworth & Bros." At times they impressed the name "ASHWORTH" into their wares. They frequently included the name of the individual pattern.

At first Messrs. Ashworths used Masons original mark "MASON'S PATENT IRONSTONE." They later added their own name and in 1891 th word "England." They employed a similar mark with the word "REAL" replacing "PATENT".[5]

### Bishop & Stonier

Located in Hanley, Powell, Bishop & Stonier produced a wide range of china and earthenware ceramics from 1878 to 1891. After 1891, the firm was renamed Bishop & Stonier and continued in similar production lines as its predecessor until 1939. According the Jewitt, Powell, Bishop & Stonier produced earthenwares of the finest quality and in every decorative style for both the home and foreign markets including Australia. The ceramic bodies were considered to be extremely hard and durable and were produced in either a pure white or an "Oriental Ivory". Decorations on dinner services, which were the company's specialities, ranged from plain white and transfer printed patterns to elaborately enamelled, painted and gilt services.

Along with their dinner services, dessert and tea services as well as toilet wares were produced. The designs of the firm were awarded medals at international exhibitions in 1862, 1869, 1875, and in Philadelphia in 1876. From 1891 to 1939, the pottery continued to produce quality earthenwares and china as Bishop & Stonier. As Bishop & Stonier the pottery produced Chelsea and Gresham patterns in Flow Blue.

GRESHAM covered cheese plate by Bishop & Stonier. 9 1/4" x 7 1/4". *Courtesy of Lucille and Norman Bagdon.*

## Marks

From 1878 to 1891, Powell, Bishop & Stonier used a number of impressed or printed marks with the initials "P. B. & S." and frequently the pattern name. In 1876, the previous partnership of Powell & Bishop registered a Caduceus trade-mark which continued to be used in marks by both Powell, Bishop & Stonier and Bishop & Stonier. In 1880, Powell, Bishop & Stonier registered a seated Asian holding an umbrella emblazoned with the ceramic body ware name "ORIENTAL IVORY" as a trade-mark which also continued to be used by Bishop & Stonier from 1891 to 1939.

Bishop & Stonier used several printed or impressed marks featuring the initials "B & S" form 1891 to 1939. The full name was also employed with some of their printed marks from 1899 to 1936. The names of both the patterns and the body type such as "IRONSTONE CHINA" were frequently used as well.[6]

## Brown-Westhead, Moore & Company

The firm occupied the prestigious Cauldon Place Works at Hanley from 1861-1904, following a long succession of successful firms. Cauldon Place was established in circa 1802 by Job Ridgway and housed the firms of John & William Ridgway, 1814-1830, John Ridgway & Company, c. 1830-1855, J. Ridgway, Bates & Company, c. 1856-1858, and Bates, Brown-Westhead, Moore & Company, c. 1858-1861.

The latest partnership continued to produce high quality wares in the tradition of their predecessors. The firm employed over 1000 people, among them leading artists and designers. They produced a wide range of earthenwares, stonewares, majolica, and some fine porcelain. These were produced as table wares, toilet sets and ornamental pieces. One of their offerings in Flow Blue was the Plymouth pattern.

PLYMOUTH toothbrush holder by Brown-Westhead, Moore, & Company, circa 1898. The toothbrush holder measures 5 3/4" high. *Courtesy of Anne & Dave Middleton, Pot O' Gold Antiques.*

Bishop & Stonier, Hanley, Staffordshire, printed Caduceus marks retreived from their predecessors Powell, Bishop & Stonier. These Caduceus marks were in use from 1891-1936. Beneath one mark is "BISTRO" and beneath the other are the firms initials "B & S." "LINCOLN" and "GRESHAM" are the pattern name. *Courtesy of Dorothy & Elmer Caskey, Trojan Antiques, Cynthiana, Kentucky 41031; Courtesy of Lucille and Norman Bagdon.*

Some of the commissions for the firm were indicative of the quality of their work. Commissions were received from Edward, Prince of Wales in 1876-1877 and the Imperial Court of Russia. They also displayed their wares at major international exhibitions including the Great International Exhibition in London in 1851 and the Centennial Exhibition in Philadelphia in 1876. In 1904 the firm became Cauldon Ltd. and later Cauldon Potteries Ltd in the 1920s.

**Marks**

Brown-Westhead, Moore & Company used a variety of marks incorporating either the full name of the firm or the initials "BWM & Co."[7]

Brown-Westhead, Moore & Company, Hanley, Staffordshire, printed mark with the company's initials and the pattern name PLYMOUTH in use from circa 1895-1904. The registration number indicates a registry date of 1898. *Courtesy of Anne & Dave Middleton, Pot O' Gold Antiques.*

## William Brownfield & Sons

William Brownfield established a pottery for himself in Cobridge in November of 1850. Here a wide variety of good quality earthenwares with printed, enamelled and gilt decorations ranging from simple to ornate were produced. The firm was very well known for their line of relief-molded ornamental jugs. In 1871 porcelain wares were added with fine quality pieces manufactured. In 1876 "& Sons" was added to the firm's name. By 1880 the firm had approximately 600 employees producing all types of decorative earthenware, particularly transfer printed wares including Flow Blue. This firm did a thriving home trade but also exported the United States, Canada and Continental Europe. Some of the more successful patterns were derived from earlier Mason patterns.

The company became Brownfield's Guild Pottery Society in 1892 and continued under this name until 1900. This company produced a Devon pattern in Flow Blue.

DEVON plate by Brownfields Guild Pottery Society Ltd., 1891-1898. 9 1/4" in diameter. *Courtesy of Louise and Charles Loehr, Louise's Old Things, Kutztown, Pennsylvania.*

## Marks

The impressed or printed marks varied and frequently bear "W.B." or "W.B. & S." initial marks or the full name in addition to the pattern name. They also employed a backstamp with a banner holding the company name and surrounding both halves of the globe.

Brownfields Guild Pottery Society Ltd. used impress and printed marks including the name or initials of the firm. One mark displays a banner with the company name over both halves of the globe beneath a pair of clasped hands.[8]

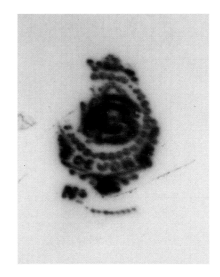

Brownfields Guild Pottery Society Ltd., Cobridge, Staffordshire, printed manufacturers' mark with interlocked central letters BPC in use from 1891-1898 and the pattern name DEVON below. *Courtesy of Louise and Charles Loehr, Louise's Old Things, Kutztown, Pennsylvania.*

## Burgess & Leigh

Burgess & Leigh (Ltd.) took over operations of the Hill Pottery in Burslem after Samuel Alcock in c. 1867 and continued production there until 1889. From there they moved to the Middleport Pottery in c. 1889 onward. They produced a wide range of earthenwares from the ordinary to the ornate for both domestic and export markets. Some of Burgess & Leigh's patterns offered in Flow Blue include Burleigh, La Hore, Napoli and Non Pariel.

## Marks

A number of impressed or printed patterns were used by the company featuring either the full name of the company or the initials B. & L. Elaborate marks include a double ribbon printed with the company name spanning the globe and another with displaying a beehive on a stand with bees, a rosebush on either side and a ribbon bearing the companys name beneath.[9]

Burgess & Leigh (Ltd.), Burslem, Staffordshire, printed initials B. & L. were in use from 1862 onward and LA HORE pattern name. *Courtesy of Lucille and Norman Bagdon.*

LA HORE sauce tureen with underplate by Burgess & Leigh (Ltd.), circa 1862. This piece is unusual as the pattern is usually seen produce by W. & E. Corn. The underplate measures 8 1/2" x 6". 5" high. *Courtesy of Lucille and Norman Bagdon.*

Burgess & Leigh (Ltd.), Burslem, Staffordshire, printed mark with England dating the mark to 1891 and later. The mark includes the NON PARIEL pattern name. *Courtesy of Anne & Dave Middleton, Pot O' Gold Antiques.*

Burgess & Leigh (Ltd.), Burslem, Staffordshire, England, printed globe manufacturers' mark in use in circa 1912 (Ltd. added in 1919) and NAPOLI pattern name. The pattern was registered with the Patent Office in London in circa 1906 according to the registration mark. *Courtesy of Louise and Charles Loehr, Louise's Old Things, Kutztown, Pennsylvania.*

NON PARIEL open vegetable dish, Burgess & Leigh (Ltd.), circa 1891. 9 1/2" x 7 1/4". *Courtesy of Dorothy & Arnold Kowalsky.*

## Cauldon Ltd.

Taking the place of Brown-Westhead, Moore & Company at the famed Cauldon Place Works in Hanley in 1905, the firm continued the practice of producing high quality earthenwares and fine porcelains. In 1920 the company title was changed to Cauldon Potteries Ltd. In 1962 the earthenware interest was acquired by Pountney & Company Ltd. The porcelain works were acquired by E. W. Brain & Company Ltd. In Flow Blue the Cauldon Ltd. produced Bentick, Candia, and Corinthian Flute patterns.

Custard cup in an unidentified pattern by Cauldon Ltd., circa 1905. 4 1/4" in diameter. *Courtesy of Dorothy & Arnold Kowalsky.*

## Marks

The name Cauldon was printed on several marks of differing designs, frequently including the pattern name. On some marks "Limited" or "Ltd." has been added. It is interesting to note that some former Ridgway and Brown-Westhead, Moore and Company marks were used with the addition of "Cauldon" or "Cauldon Ltd." and "England".[10]

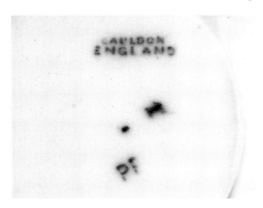

Cauldon Ltd., Hanley, Staffordshire, printed mark in use from 1905 to 1920. On some marks "Ltd." or "Limited" were added to the mark. *Courtesy of Dorothy & Arnold Kowalsky.*

## Edward Challinor

"The earthenware is of the ordinary common quality, specially designed and well adapted for the various markets to which it is sent." — Llewellynn Jewitt, 1877

Established at the Pinnock Works, Tunstall in 1842 until 1867. Edward Challinor and E. Challinor and Company at the Fenton Potteries in Fenton from 1853-1867, followed by E. & C. Challinor at the Fenton Pottery in Fenton produced white granite, transfer printed, flown, and sponged for the export market. Tea, coffee, breakfast, and dinner services were produced along with toilet sets and other useful domestic articles.

Between 1842 and 1867 Edward Challinor produced Flow Blue in the Cabul, Dahlia, Kin-Shan, Lozern, Pelew and Shell patterns. The Official Catalogue of the Great Exhibition of 1851 stated that at the exhibition he presented "Basins, closet utensils, etc. in flown mulberry marble to match."

KIN SHAN teapot by Edward Challinor, c. 1855. 9 1/2" high to the spoout. *Courtesy of Lucille and Norman Bagdon.*

## Marks

Edward Challinor used several printed marks with the company name or initials and with the pattern name often included. This pattern holds true for E. Challinor & Company (1853-1862) and E. & C. Challinor (1862-1891).[11]

Edward Challinor, Tunstall and Fenton, Staffordshire, printed E. C. mark in use from 1842-1867 and the SHELL pattern name. *Courtesy of Joseph Nigro & Ralph Wick, Old Things Made New Again.*

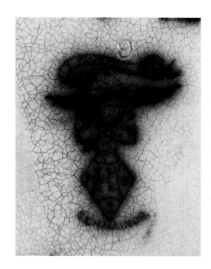

Edward Challinor & Company, Tunstall and Fenton, Staffordshire, printed E. Challinor mark in use from 1842-1867 and the CABUL pattern name. The pattern was registered with the Patent Office in London in circa 1847 according to the registration mark. *Courtesy of Lucille and Norman Bagdon.*

quality transfer printed designs. Much of Clementson's production was exported to America and Canada. Joseph Clementson produced a Chusan pattern in Flow Blue. Clementson retired from business in 1867 and died in 1871. His sons succeeded him and traded as "Clementson Brothers" until 1916.

## Marks

Several printed marks bearing the name "J. CLEMENTSON" or the initials "J.C." are known. One mark used from 1840 onward has the Phoenix bird with the name "J. CLEMENTSON" underneath it.[12]

Edward Challinor & Company, Fenton, Staffordshire, printed E.C. & Co. mark in use from 1853-1860 with the KIN-SHAN pattern name. *Courtesy of Lucille and Norman Bagdon.*

Joseph Clementson, Shelton, Hanley, Staffordshire, printed J. Clementson and Phoenix bird mark in use from 1840 onward. CHUSAN is the pattern name. *Courtesy of Lucille and Norman Bagdon.*

## Joseph Clementson

Joseph Clementson became the sole proprietor of the Phoenix Works in Shelton, Hanley in c. 1839 after a period of joint ownership as Reed & Clementson which began in 1832. Jewitt states that Clementson gained sole proprietorship shortly after the 1832 date. The works prospered and were expanded in 1845. In 1856 he purchased the Bell Works previously occupied by William Ridgway. Clementsons' firm produced granite wares with white surfaces and with painted or printed decoration. The firm was known for high

## W.T. Copeland (& Sons)

"The list of [William T.] Copeland's productions comprises all classes of goods — from the statuary porcelain figures and the elaborately decorated vase, to the commonest article of earthenware — manufactured for exportation by tens of thousands." — The Art Journal Illustrated Catalogue, 1851

In June of 1847, William Taylor Copeland's partner of fourteen years, Thomas Garrett, retired. Copeland purchased the entire firm, the Spode Works founded by Josiah Spode in the late eighteenth century at Stoke, for himself. While changing the name of the firm from Copeland & Garrett to W.T. Copeland, he persisted in the tradition of Spode and Copeland & Garrett in the production of high quality porcelain and a wide range of earthenwares worthy of exportation. W.T. Copeland produced a flowing Marble pattern.

Copeland became Minton's greatest rival at Stoke, employing over 800 people by 1861. Copeland's product was highly respected, the firm enjoyed royal patronage — providing a special dessert service for the Prince of Wales in 1866, and was involved in all major international exhibitions.

CHUSAN plate by Joseph Clementson, dating to circa 1850. 7 1/4" diameter plate. *Courtesy of Anne & Dave Middleton, Pot O' Gold Antiques.*

A Rose pattern pedestalled cake stand by Copeland and Garrett, dating from 1835-1840. 11 1/2" in diameter and 2 1/2" high. *Courtesy of Dorothy & Arnold Kowalsky.*

In 1877 Jewitt proclaimed that for breakfast, dinner, dessert, tea and toilet services the firm was among the best. A further note of interest from Jewitt concerns a particular body produced by Copeland, "One of the greatest improvements effected ... in ordinary earthenware is the production of ... an 'Ivory-tinted body.' ... In the dinner and dessert services the delicate, soft, warm tone of the ivory tint ... has a charming effect when 'set' out on the white linen cloth ..."

Unidentified pattern plate by W.T. Copeland, dating from 1875. 10 1/4". *Courtesy of Louise and Charles Loehr, Louise's Old Things, Kutztown, Pennsylvania.*

In about 1867 his four sons entered the firm as partners, changing the name to W.T. Copeland & Sons. The Copeland company would continue long after William Copeland's death, reverting to the Spode Ltd. name in 1970.

## Marks

Copeland's wares usually bear clear name-marks and they may be often be dated within narrow limits. There are a wide range of designs in the marks. Printed and impressed marks are both to be found. Several include the phrase "LATE SPODE" until 1867, reminding the consumer of the potteries distinguished past. In 1867 Copeland's four sons arrive and the name-mark is changed to "W.T. COPELAND·& SONS".

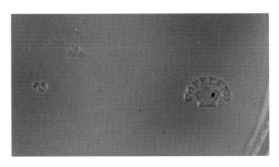

Copeland and Garrett, Stoke, Staffordshire, this printed mark reading COPELAND AND GARRETT was in use from circa 1833-1847. *Courtesy of Dorothy & Arnold Kowalsky.*

Copeland and Garrett produced several printed marks with either the initials C. & G. or the full "COPELAND & GARRETT" name. They marked the vast majority of their wares. Several printed marks incorporate the pattern name or body type. The marks date from 1833-1847.[13]

W. T. Copeland (& Sons Ltd.), Stoke, Staffordshire, COPELAND and crown impressed mark in use in 1875. The impressed date mark S 75 shows the month letter code and the last two digits of the year, in this case 1875. *Courtesy of Louise and Charles Loehr, Louise's Old Things, Kutztown, Pennsylvania.*

## Davenport

"Some of the cups ... are of elegant form, and those in blue and white, whether in pencilled, ordinary transfer printing or 'flown', are highly successful." — Llewellynn Jewitt, 1877

John Davenport bought and enlarged the Unicorn Bank works in 1793 in Longport, Staffordshire. Davenport began by producing cream-colored earthenware with well painted and fine blue transfer printed designs. Later stone china would be added to the earthenwares.

By circa 1805 Davenport was producing porcelain which quickly lead to the production of expensive fine porcelain lines. By 1810 Davenport was producing a wide range of domestic wares, vases and a few figurines.

An dynamic export trade began in c. 1815. Ironstone bodies were produced in large quantities until the 1880s, destined for American shores.

John Davenport retired a wealthy man in 1832. At that time his firm employed in excess of 1400 people. His sons carried the business forward until 1887. Beginning c. 1830 the firm was using a variety of ground colors, heavy gilding, and elaborate landscapes, well crafted flowers, and still lifes. In 1858 William Davenport took over the business. Davenport dessert services from the 1850s through the 1870s were highly regarded. During the final decades, under Henry Davenport, Japanese-style patterns were in vogue at Davenport. The firm continued until 1881, when the firm became a private company, "Davenport & Company". The company finally closed in 1887.

In Flow Blue Davenport produced Amoy, Cypress, Damask, Ivy, Madras, Marble, Rose and Vine Border patterns.

## Marks

The anchor is the distinguishing feature of the Davenport marks. Accompanying the anchor at times are the last two digits of the year place on either side of the anchor. The crown was first used on a royal service for William IV. Davenport used a variety of printed and impressed marks including the name of the firm and often the pattern name.[14]

Davenport, Longport, Staffordshire, impressed DAVENPORT and anchor mark. The upper case manufacturers' name came into use in 1805 and the anchor in many cases on this mark has the last two digits of the year impressed on either side of the anchor itself. *Courtesy of Dorothy & Arnold Kowalsky.*

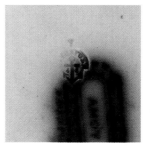

Davenport, Longport, Staffordshire, on either side of the impressed anchor are the digits 44, indicating the year 1844. *Courtesy of Anne & Dave Middleton, Pot O' Gold Antiques.*

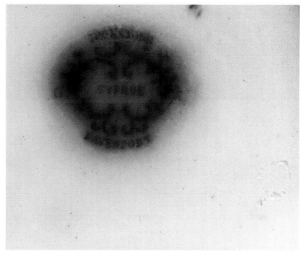

Davenport, Longport, Staffordshire, printed mark with the name DAVENPORT was in use in a variety of forms from 1820 to 1860. An impressed anchor manufacturers' mark found on the piece as well narrows the date for this particular piece to 1848. This mark also presents the printed pattern name CYPRUS and the body ware type IRONSTONE. *Courtesy of Joseph Nigro & Ralph Wick, Old Things Made New Again.*

MADRAS compote by Davenport (circa 1793-1887), impressed 1841. 10 1/4" in diameter and 5 1/2" high. *Courtesy of Lucille and Norman Bagdon.*

## Thomas Dimmock

Thomas Dimmock established himself in Shelton in c. 1828 producing earthenwares considered by the jury at the Great Exhibition of 1851 in London to be of first-rate quality. His patterns were admired for their neatness and good taste, for the general excellence of his wares and for "...the agreeable effect of his 'flowing blue'". Dimmock's efforts were awarded a prize medal. Thomas Dimmock's flowing blue patterns included Bamboo, Chinese, Ivy, Lily, and Rhine. The firm remained in business until 1859.

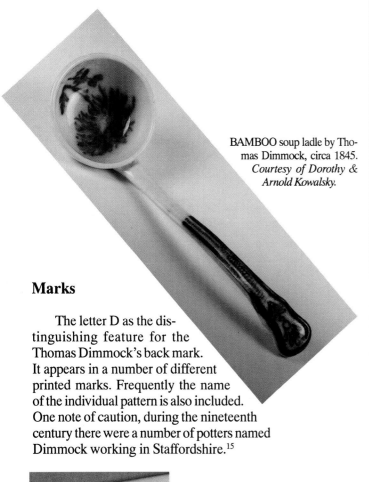

BAMBOO soup ladle by Thomas Dimmock, circa 1845. *Courtesy of Dorothy & Arnold Kowalsky.*

### Marks

The letter D as the distinguishing feature for the Thomas Dimmock's back mark. It appears in a number of different printed marks. Frequently the name of the individual pattern is also included. One note of caution, during the nineteenth century there were a number of potters named Dimmock working in Staffordshire.[15]

Thomas Dimmock & Company, Shelton, Staffordshire, printed manufacturers' marks featuring the initial D which was in use by the firm from circa 1828 to 1859. The pattern names CHINESE and LILY are included along with the body ware type KAOLIN WARE. The registration mark indicates the design LILY was registered in 1844. *Courtesy of Lucille and Norman Bagdon; Courtesy of Joseph Nigro & Ralph Wick, Old Things Made New Again.*

## Doulton & Company (Ltd.)

"Messrs. Doulton produce extensively all the usual services and domestic articles in every class and variety of decoration, and suitable for every market and every household."
— Llewellynn Jewitt, 1877

Corset Pitcher with an unidentified pattern by Doulton & Company (Ltd.), dating from 1891-1902. 8 3/4" high. *Courtesy of Louise and Charles Loehr, Louise's Old Things, Kutztown, Pennsylvania.*

Doulton & Company was established in Lambeth in the mid-1850s following the dissolution of Doulton & Watts and firms owned by brothers Henry and John Doulton. Production of utilitarian stoneware which had begun in c. 1815 continued. Earthenwares were produced from 1872 onward. A particularly fine bodied ivory earthenware was produced from c. 1892-1900. This was christened Crown Lambeth and was first exhibited in 1893 in Chicago. Large scale production of table services and other domestic wares included numerous pattern series which would remain in production for extended periods. Doulton was known for a wide range of styles. Art Nouveau influences may be found in Doulton wares. Patterns were also adapted from illustrators works, hunt scenes, cartoons, historical views, literary works, sports, floral arrangements and animal studies. Production ceased in Lambeth in 1956.

In c. 1882 Doulton and Company established themselves in Nile Street in Burslem as well. At the former works of Pinder Bourne & Company, Doulton produced a wide range of earthenwares and porcelains. The quality of the earthenware was superior to most. Doulton kept a number of highly skilled artisans on staff to ensure the quality of their wares.

Designs by Doulton were influenced by Japanese art as well. Llewellynn Jewitt refered admiringly to this while displaying a certain ambivilence towards the originators of the style. Jewitt remarked that Doulton produced "... original designs imbued with the quaint ideas of the Japanese artists, rendered more graceful and acceptable by the refinement of feeling of the English mind ..." In Flow Blue the English minds at Doulton produced Adelaide, Galleon, Geneva, Glorie De Dijon, Iris, Madras, Melrose, Watteau and Willow patterns.

In 1955 Doulton & Company of Burslem was retitled Doulton Fine China Ltd. and continues production today.

Doulton & Co. (Ltd.), Burslem, Staffordshire, printed manufacturers' mark dating from circa 1882-1902. England was added in 1891. This mark was used on bone china and more expensive earthenwares. *Courtesy of Louise and Charles Loehr, Louise's Old Things, Kutztown, Pennsylvania.*

Doulton & Co. (Ltd.), Burslem, Staffordshire, printed manufacturers' mark dating from circa 1901 to 1922. The mark was introduced to signify the grant of the Royal Warrant by King Edward VII together with the right to use the word ROYAL on Doulton products. The pattern name MADRAS is printed below the mark. *Courtesy of Dorothy & Arnold Kowalsky.*

MADRAS charger by Doulton and Company, circa 1900. 13 1/2" diameter. *Courtesy of Dorothy & Arnold Kowalsky.*

## Marks

Doulton & Company Ltd. of Lambeth used a variety of printed marks including the name "DOULTON" and the Lambeth location in the mark. Both impressed and printed marks were used. Pattern names were frequently included.

Doulton & Company Ltd. of Burslem also produced a variety of impressed and printed marks including the name and town. The word "England" was added to the mark in 1891 and "Made in England" in c. 1930. The name "ROYAL DOULTON" appears around four interlace Ds, frequently beneath a lion and usually on a coronet, from 1902. Again, the pattern name is often included.[16]

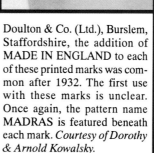

Doulton & Co. (Ltd.), Burslem, Staffordshire, the addition of MADE IN ENGLAND to each of these printed marks was common after 1932. The first use with these marks is unclear. Once again, the pattern name MADRAS is featured beneath each mark. *Courtesy of Dorothy & Arnold Kowalsky.*

## James Edwards

James Edwards began work at Dale Hall in Burslem in 1842. He produced earthenwares and a high quality ironstone christened granite ware. He maintained a brisk export business. James Edwards brought his son Richard into the business in 1851 and changed the name of the establishment to "James Edwards & Son." In 1851 at the Great Exhibition Edwards also received both a medal and a certificate of merit for "beauty of form and excellence of goods exhibited." Edwards attended the international exhibitions regularly. James Edwards retired in 1867. His son Richard continued the works until 1882 when it was purchased by Knapper & Blackhurst.

James Edwards contributions to Flow Blue included the patterns Cabul, Canton, and Chinese Bells.

EXCELSIOR sweetmeat dish by Thomas Fell, circa 1850. 11 1/2" x 9 1/4" x 6" high. *Courtesy of Joseph Nigro & Ralph Wick, Old Things Made New Again.*

CANTON teapot, sugar bowl and cremer by James Edwards, circa 1850. Teapot, sugar and creamer, The teapot measures 9 1/4" high, the sugar bowl 8 1/4" high, and the creamer 5 1/2" high. *Courtesy of Lucille and Norman Bagdon.*

## Marks

Thomas Fell used several impressed or printed marks featuring either the initials "F. & Co.", "T.F. & Co." or the name of the firm.[18]

Thomas Fell & Company, Newcastle upon Tyne, Northumberland, printed T.F. & Co. mark in use from circa 1830 to 1890. *Courtesy of Joseph Nigro & Ralph Wick, Old Things Made New Again.*

## Marks

James Edwards impressed and printed marks include the company initials or full name on a variety of marks. The initials D.H., for Dale Hall, are often present.[17]

## Thomas Fell & Company

Thomas Fell's firm produced earthenwares out of St. Peter's Pottery, Newcastle upon Tyne, Northumberland from 1817 to 1890. Over the course of its career, the company exported Flow Blue to America in Excelsior and Japan patterns. In 1851 Thomas Fell & Company attended the Great Exhibition in London. Of their appearance the Official Catalogue reported tersely, "Specimens of common earthenware."

## The Furnivals

Jacob Furnival & Company, the predecessor of Thomas Furnival & Sons was in business in Cobridge from c. 1845 to 1870. The company produced hard-bodied earthenwares for the export market including Flow Blue in Gothic and Shanghae patterns.

Thomas Furnival & Company, formerly Jacob & Thomas Furnival (c. 1843), was established in Hanley in c. 1844 and had a short run under that name which ended in 1846. Producing hard-bodied earthenwares for the export market as well, Thomas Furnival & Company is attributed with producing Indian Jar, Rhone and Tivoli patterns in Flow Blue.

GOTHIC teapot by Jacob Furnival, circa 1850. 8 1/2" high. *Courtesy of Louise and Charles Loehr, Louise's Old Things, Kutztown, Pennsylvania.*

Furnival & Sons combined transfer printing with hand painting, enamelling and gilding in some of their services. "Swan" and "Nautilus" were considered to be among their most successful toilet services. In Flow Blue Thomas Furnival & Sons produced the Ceylon pattern. After 1890, renamed Furnivals, the company went on to produce Flow Blue in Bouquet, Carnation, and Versailles patterns.

## Marks

Jacob Furnival & Company employed several printed marks with the initials "J F & CO." and the pattern name from c. 1845-1870.

Jacob Furnival & Company, Cobridge, Staffordshire, printed mark with the "J F & CO." initials in use from circa 1845-1870 and the GOTHIC pattern name. *Courtesy of Lucille and Norman Bagdon.*

Jacob & Thomas Furnival used a printed mark featuring the Royal Arms and the initials "J & T F", c. 1843.

Thomas Furnival & Company printed several marks with different designs. The initials "T. F. & CO." were employed. These marks frequently included pattern names and were used from c. 1844-1846.

Thomas Furnival & Sons produced a variety of marks. Printed monogram and printed Royal Arms marks were employed from 1871-1890 and a printed or impressed crest mark was registered in 1878. The marks featured either the initials of the firm with the words "& Sons" or the full name of the firm. Frequently pattern names were included with the marks.[19]

RHONE platter by Thomas Furnival and Company, circa 1844-1846. 13 1/4" x 10 1/2". *Courtesy of Dorothy & Arnold Kowalsky.*

In 1877 Thomas Furnival & Sons was considered to be an old, established firm with a high ranking among manufacturers of white granite, ironstone, and decorated toilet wares for the export markets in the United States, Canada and Europe. Furnival & Sons, located in Cobridge, occupied two factories previously owned by the Adams and Blackwell potteries. This firm was in production under the Thomas Furnival & Sons name from 1871 to 1890. The name was changed to Furnivals (Ltd.) in 1890.

Thomas Furnival & Company, Hanley, Staffordshire, printed T. F. & Co. manufacturers' mark, circa 1844-46 and RHONE pattern name. *Courtesy of Louise and Charles Loehr, Louise's Old Things, Kutztown, Pennsylvania.*

Thomas Furnival & Company, Hanley, Staffordshire, another printed T. F. & Co. manufacturers' mark, circa 1844-46 and TIVOLI pattern name. *Courtesy of Dorothy & Arnold Kowalsky.*

## W. H. Grindley & Company (Ltd.)

Established in the New Field Pottery, Tunstall in c. 1880, W. H. Grindley & Company produced earthenwares and ironstones. They produced their wares at the New Field Pottery until 1891 and continuing with the Woodland Pottery in Tunstall from 1891 forward. In 1960 the firm was purchased by Alfred Clough Ltd.

During the last quarter of the nineteenth and the first quarter of the twentieth centuries, W. H. Grindley & Company produced Flow Blue popular in the American market. Flow Blue patterns produced by the firm include Alaska, Albany, Argyle, Ashburton, Baltic, Beaufort, Blue Rose, Clarence, Clover, Duchess, Florida, Gironde, Grace, Haddon, The Hofburg, Idris, Keele, Le Pavot, Lorne, Lotus, Marachal Neil, Marguerite, Marie, The Marquis, Melbourne, Osborne, Poppy, Portman, Rose and Shanghai.

ALASKA soup bowl by W.H. Grindley & Company, 1891, 8 7/8" in diameter with flanch. *Courtesy of Dorothy & Arnold Kowalsky.*

## Marks

A variety of printed marks were employed by the firm. The marks featured here are common to Flow Blue. The name of the company is present and "Ltd." was added from 1925 onward. Pattern names are frequently printed with the marks.[20]

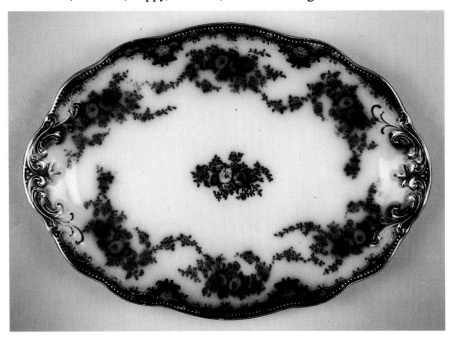

FLORIDA platter with gold trim by W.H. Grindley & Company, circa 1891. 16" x 11 5/8". *Courtesy of Dorothy & Arnold Kowalsky.*

W.H. Grindley & Company, Tunstall, Staffordshire, printed W.H. GRINDLEY & CO. manufacturers' mark in use from circa 1880 to 1914. This mark features the word ENGLAND after the company name, dating it to 1891 and after. Earlier marks had Tunstall following the company name. The pattern name MARGUERITE is in the banner above the globe. *Courtesy of Anne & Dave Middleton, Pot O' Gold Antiques.*

W.H. Grindley & Company, Tunstall, Staffordshire, printed W.H. GRINDLEY & CO. manufacturers' mark in use from circa 1914 to 1925. THE REGAL pattern name is above the mark. *Courtesy of Dorothy & Arnold Kowalsky.*

FLORIDA soup bowls, cup and saucer, berry dish and butter pat by Johnson Brothers, circa 1900. The largest soup bowls measure 8 7/8" and 7 7/8" in diameter, the soup without a flanch measures 7 1/4" in diameter, and the berry dish measures 4 7/8" in diameter. *Courtesy of Dorothy & Arnold Kowalsky.*

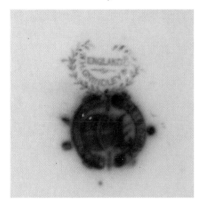

At times both manufacturers' marks appear together. The pattern name MELBOURNE is present in the globe mark. *Courtesy of Dorothy & Arnold Kowalsky.*

## Johnson Brothers Ltd.

Johnson Brothers Ltd, formerly J.W. Pankhurst & Company, began production at Hanley Pottery in Hanley in 1877. The company continues in operation. Johnson Brothers Ltd. operated a pottery in Tunstall from c. 1899-1913 as well. The firm produced a variety of earthenwares, not the least of which was Flow Blue for the export market. Flow Blue patterns produced included Blue Danube, Clarissa, Clayton, Eclipse, Florida, Georgia, Holland, Jewel, Kenworth, Mongolia, Normandy, Oxford, Peach, Richmond, Savoy, Stanley, and Warwick.

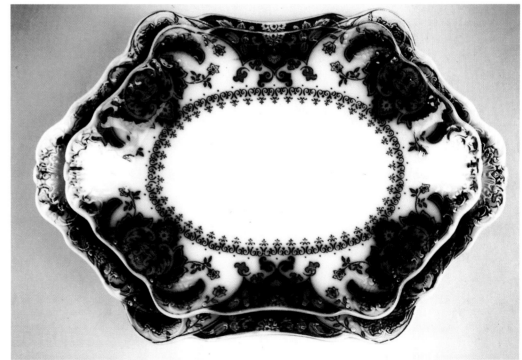

FLORIDA nested platters by Johnson Brothers, circa 1900. 16 1/2" x 11 1/4" and 14 1/2" x 10" platters. *Courtesy of Dorothy & Arnold Kowalsky.*

## Marks

Several printed or impressed marks are found carrying the "Johnson Bros." name and frequently the name of the pattern.[21]

Johnson Brothers Ltd., Hanley and Tunstall, Staffordshire, printed crown mark with "JOHNSON BROS." manufacturers' name and the "FLORIDA" pattern name, circa 1900+. *Courtesy of Dorothy & Arnold Kowalsky.*

Johnson Brothers Ltd., Hanley and Tunstall, Staffordshire, printed crown mark with "JOHNSON BROS." manufacturers' name and "ROYSTON" pattern name, circa 1913+. *Courtesy of Louise and Charles Loehr, Louise's Old Things, Kutztown, Pennsylvania.*

## John Maddock

John Maddock established himself at New Castle Street in Burslem, first in two partnerships before c. 1842, then by himself and finally with his sons in 1855. Maddock's first partnership was with James Edwards prior to 1839 and was brief. James Edwards went on to establish his own

pottery. From 1839 to c. 1842, in another short lived partnership the pottery was named Maddock & Seddon. From c. 1842 to 1855 John Maddock continued on his own. In 1855, Maddock took his sons into partnership and changed the name of the firm to John Maddock & Sons. The term "Ltd." was added to the name after 1896. The firm continues during the twentieth century.

John Maddock's firms produced a variety of earthenwares over the years. Of the potteries later work, Jewitt states, "John Maddock and Son manufacture white graniteware for the American market to a large extent." No mention was made of the quality of the product. As John Maddock & Sons, the pottery produced the Hindustan pattern in Flow Blue.

HINDUSTAN platter by John Maddock, circa 1850. 15 7/8" x 12 3/8". *Courtesy of Dorothy & Arnold Kowalsky.*

## Marks

Maddock & Seddon produced several printed marks featuring the initials of the firm "M. & S." Names of patterns were often included as well as the name of the ware type such as "Stone China."

John Maddock used the initial "M" or the name "MADDOCK" in several printed marks, at least one of which was used in his previous association with Seddon. These marks were used from c. 1839-1842 and may include pattern names and the name of the ware type such as "Ironstone China".

John Maddock & Sons (Ltd.) employed a variety of printed and impressed marks including the full name of the firm "John Maddock & Sons" or simply the last name "Maddock". After 1896 "Ltd." was added to the mark. Again pattern names and ware types are often included.[22]

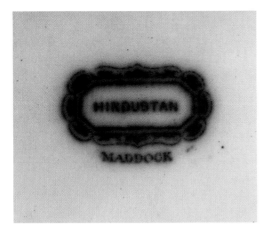

John Maddock, Burslem, Staffordshire, printed manu-facturers' mark in use from 1842-1855 and the HINDUSTAN pattern name. *Courtesy of Dorothy & Arnold Kowalsky.*

John Maddock, Burslem, Staffordshire, impressed manufacturers' mark in use from 1842-1855. After 1855 "& Son" was added to the mark. The name of the body type of the ware "IRONSTONE CHINA" was included. *Courtesy of Dorothy & Arnold Kowalsky.*

In 1877, looking back on the Mayers, Jewitt considered them, "... exceedingly clever potters." Jewitt spoke highly of the quality of their wares as well, stating, "The dinner plates, dishes, etc. of Messrs. Mayer were characterised by an excellent 'fit' in nesting, lightness of body, and neatness of finish." In Flow Blue, the Mayers production included such patterns as Arabesque, Formosa, Grecian Scroll, and Oregon.

ARABESQUE platter by T.J. & J. Mayer, circa 1845. 20 1/4" x 15 3/4". *Courtesy of Anne & Dave Middleton, Pot O' Gold Antiques.*

## Thomas, John & Joseph Mayer

"Exhibited a most interesting assortment of articles illustrative of the ordinary course of their trade, which is principally connected with the markets of the American Continent. Messrs. Mayer adapt their excellent material to every variety of useful purpose." — Juried Results of the Great International Exhibition of 1851.

Producing, among others, well received earthenwares, china, and Parian wares from their Furlong Works and Dale Hall Pottery in Burslem, from 1843 to 1855, Thomas, John & Joseph Mayer participated in the Exhibitions of 1851, 1853 and 1855. They presented table wares, toilette wares and dish covers at the 1851 Exhibition which were considered eminently suitable for the export trade. The jury awarded them a medal for their efforts.

ARABESQUE teapot by T.J.&J. Mayer, circa 1845. 8 1/2" high. *Courtesy of Lucille and Norman Bagdon.*

## Marks

The name "T. J. & J. Mayer" was employed on several printed marks. Pattern names were frequently included. "Mayer Bros." was also used.[23]

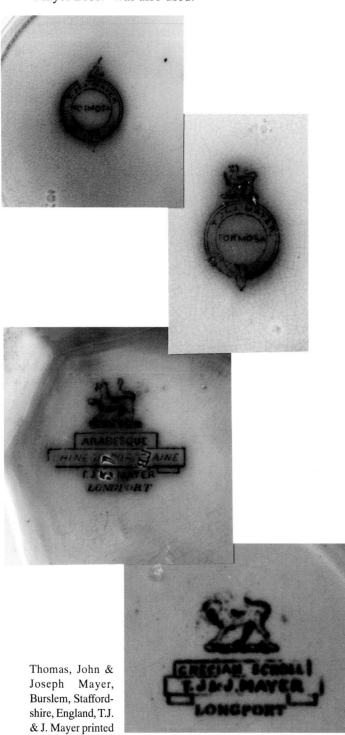

Thomas, John & Joseph Mayer, Burslem, Staffordshire, England, T.J. & J. Mayer printed manufacturers' marks used from 1843-1855 with FORMOSA, GRECIAN SCROLL, and ARABESQUE pattern names. *Courtesy of Louise & Charles Loehr, Louise's Old Things, Kutztown, Pennsylvania; Courtesy of Lucille and Norman Bagdon; Courtesy of Anne & Dave Middleton, Pot O' Gold Antiques; Courtesy of Louise and Charles Loehr, Louise's Old Things, Kutztown, Pennsylvania.*

## The Meakin Family

Alfred Meakin established himself in 1875, producing "...the ordinary classes of earthenware goods" at the Royal Albert and Victoria and Highgate Potteries in Tunstall. In c. 1913 the firm was renamed "Alfred Meakin Ltd." Cambridge, Devon, Kelvin, Richmond, and Verona patterns were produced in Flow Blue by the Alfred Meakin works.

James and George Meakin produced earthenwares, ironstones and other wares at the Eagle Pottery and Eastwood Works in Hanley. They took control of the family works after their father, James Meakin, retired in 1852. The Eagle Pottery was built in 1859 as business expanded and was enlarged in 1868. James and George Meakin produced the Colonial pattern in Flow Blue.

## Marks

The name "Alfred Meakin" is featured in a variety of printed or impressed marks. "Ltd." was added after 1897 and dropped again after 1930.

The brothers James and George Meakin used "J. & G. Meakin" with a number of impressed or printed marks from 1851 to the present day. The Royal Arms are found on many marks as are the pattern names.[24]

## The Meigh Family

"The manufactory of Messrs. Charles Meigh & Sons ... is one of the largest and oldest in the pottery district ... in proof of its extent ... upward of 700 hands are employed there in the various departments; that more than 250 tons of coal are consumed every week; and that, during the same short space of time, 80 tons of clay are made into their various articles of manufacture." — The Art Journal, 1851.

Job Meigh built the Old Hall Pottery in Hanley in c. 1770, potting cream-colored and red earthenwares. The works ran uninterrupted in the family until 1861. Job Meigh took his son Charles into the business in around 1812 and the firm Job Meigh & Sons produced wares until 1834. The pottery traded under the name Charles Meigh from 1835-1849. Charles then took his son, also Charles, into the business. After a brief stint as Charles Meigh, Son & Pankhurst in a brief partnership from 1849-1851, the name was changed to Charles Meigh & Son from 1851 to 1861. In 1861 Charles Meigh transferred the business to a limited liability company known as "The Old Hall Earthenware Company."

Charles Meigh built the pottery into a large establishment as The Art Journal indicated. The pottery produced high quality earthenwares dubbed "opaque porcelain" decorated largely in blue and white transfer printed patterns. Their wares ranged from dinner, dessert, tea, and breakfast services to toilet articles. Ornamentation varied from plain to decorative. The company exhibited a range of quality earthenwares including large vases at the 1851 Exhibition. Much of Charles Meigh & Son's product was exported to the United States, France and Germany.

Of Charles Meigh & Sons patterns, Jewitt exclaimed, "Many of the patterns of dinner services are of great beauty and elegance." Flow Blue patterns produced by Charles Meigh include Hong Kong, Indian, and Troy. Patterns in Flow Blue by Charles Meigh & Sons include Kelvin, Sphinx and Troy.

## Marks

Job Meigh used an impressed name mark "MEIGH" from 1805-1834, an impressed or printed "OLD HALL" mark in 1805 and the initials "J. M. & S." when his son Charles joined him in c. 1812. This mark was used, at times in conjunction with a printed design until 1834.

Charles Meigh from 1835-1849 created many impressed marks featuring his full name. The majority of Charles Meigh's printed marks used the initials "C. M." with the pattern name and body type. Many marks included the Royal Arms.

TROY underplate by Charles Meigh, circa 1840, 10 1/4" x 8 1/2". *Courtesy of Joseph Nigro & Ralph Wick, Old Things Made New Again.*

Charles Meigh, Hanley, Staffordshire, printed C. M. manufacturers' mark in use from 1835-1849 with SPHINX pattern name. *Courtesy of Lucille and Norman Bagdon.*

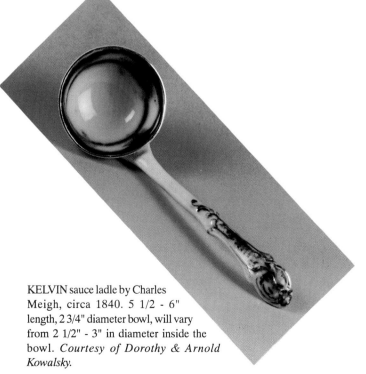

KELVIN sauce ladle by Charles Meigh, circa 1840. 5 1/2 - 6" length, 2 3/4" diameter bowl, will vary from 2 1/2" - 3" in diameter inside the bowl. *Courtesy of Dorothy & Arnold Kowalsky.*

Charles Meigh, Hanley, Staffordshire, printed C. M. manufacturers' mark in use from 1835-1849 with TROY pattern name. Impressed body ware type "IMPROVED STONE CHINA." *Courtesy of Joseph Nigro & Ralph Wick, Old Things Made New Again.*

When Charle Meigh's son Charles joined the firm in 1851 the initials on the variety of printed marks employed were changed to "C. M. & S." or "M. & S." This would continue until 1861. Pattern names and body types were frequently included. The Royal Arms were incorporated into several marks.[25]

## Minton

"Of the variety of productions of Minton's works in former and present times it is impossible to speak in detail. So varied, so distinct, and so extensive are they in material, in body, in style, in decoration, and in uses, that anything like a detailed account becomes impossible." — Llewellynn Jewitt, 1877

Founded at Stoke-on-Trent by Thomas Minton in 1793, the Minton factory has a tradition of producing high quality and widely varied ceramics which continues today. Thomas' son Herbert took over the works in 1836, maintained control until 1858, greatly expanding and modernizing the factory and its range of wares during his tenure.

Among Thomas Minton's early contributions were tablewares in blue transfer printed cream-colored earthenwares. Thomas widened his scope. The firm's tablewares were produced in semi-porcelain bodies as well as iron-stone china, white eathenware and bone china. Transfer printes included oriental, Renaissance and Gothic patterns which were designed in the early nineteenth century and continued to be used throughout the century. Under Herbert Minton, the factory kept tablewares as their mainstay but branched out into other areas as well, producing fine porcelain, parian figures, majolica, porcelains decorated by foreign artists in the Sèvres-style, and Pâte-sur-Pâte vases. To insure high quality wares, Minton's employed the most skilled artisans. Herbert Minton saw that the firm competed, and won high honors regularly, at the international exhibitions, beginning with the Great Exhibition of 1851 where he introduced majolica.

One of the effects of Herbert Mintons' modernization of the plant was to lower his cost of production of formerly expensive table services without cheapening the appearance. Herbert Minton also produced blue transfer printed wares with improved technique and quality at a time when the quality of many potters transfer prints were in decline. The British critics looked down their collective noses at Flow Blue. Herbert Minton, well aware of the negative attitude at home, defended his flowing wares to retailers Messrs. Moilliet & Gem on January 5, 1848 after they had commented positively on the lack of flow among some of his wares in the Anemone pattern. Minton explained, "... it is the flow that imparts the fine rich appearance to the color, though at the same time it occasionally produces indistinctions in the pattern. ... Anemone is engraved especially as a flown pattern ..."

ANEMONE soup tureen by Minton. The pattern was introduced in the 1830s and popular until the 1870s. Herbert Minton stated that the ANEMONE patten was designed specifically to be a flowing pattern. Handle to handle, 11 5/8", 11" in diameter, 11" high. *Courtesy of Dorothy & Arnold Kowalsky.*

Of the Minton pottery's contribution to Flow Blue, their patterns included Amherst Japan, Anemonie, Osaka, and Passion Flower.

OSAKA Biscuit jar by Minton. Electroplating began in the 1840s. Some lids may be marked, others may not. Silver marks on collar. Height 5 3/4" and 4 3/4" in diameter. *Courtesy of Dorothy & Arnold Kowalsky.*

PASSION FLOWER pepper pot by Minton. 3 1/4" high. *Courtesy of Lucille and Norman Bagdon.*

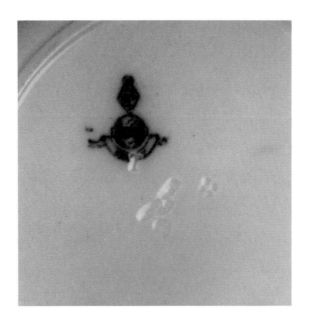

## Marks

From 1793 to 1806, Thomas Minton was in partnership with Joseph Poulson, a ceramicist, and traded under the name Minton & Poulson. The firm then traded under the names Minton & Boyle until 1836, Herbert Minton & Company until 1841, Minton & Company until 1845 and Mintons Ltd. beginning in 1873.

A wide variety of impressed and printed marks were used incorporating the "MINTON" name. The impressed mark read as "MINTONS" beginning in 1873. The impressed initials "B.B." were used during the mid-nineteenth century to indicated Best Body. Year cyphers were also employed by the firm from 1842 on. These marks occur in threesomes featuring a month letter, potter's mark and the year cypher.[26]

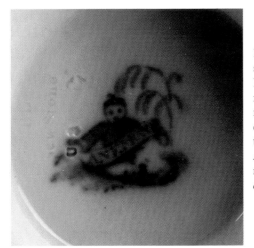

BB impressed in the base signify Minton's Best Body ware. This designation was used on mid-nineteenth century earthenwares. Occurring with this is the printed ANEMONE pattern name. *Courtesy of Dorothy & Arnold Kowalsky.*

Minton, Stoke, Staffordshire, printed MINTON manufacturers' mark in use from circa 1873 onward. In 1891 "England" was added beneath the mark, changing to "Made in England" from circa 1902-1911. *Courtesy of Dorothy & Arnold Kowalsky.*

Mintons, Stoke, Staffordshire, MINTONS printed manufacturers' mark in use from circa 1873 to 1891. The diamond shaped registration mark is too flown to be legible, although it provides some hint as these registration marks ceased to be used in 1883. The impressed MINTONS mark began to be used in 1873 as well. The year cypher (small circle surrounding a box) indicates a 1877 date. *Courtesy of Louise and Charles Loehr, Louise's Old Things, Kutztown, Pennsylvania.*

## New Wharf Pottery Company

New Wharf Pottery Company operated out of New Street, Burslem from 1878 to 1894. In 1894 the firm was purchased by Wood & Son. New Wharf Pottery produced earthenwares and their contributions to Flow Blue included the Conway, Knox, Lancaster and Waldorf patterns.

## Marks

New Wharf Pottery Company produced several printed marks with either the initials "N. W. P. CO." or the name "New Wharf Pottery". The initial marks also included the initial "B." or the full name of the town "BURSLEM" at times. Individual pattern names were often included with the marks.[27]

## Podmore, Walker & Company

The company began their operations in Tunstall in 1834 as Podmore, Walker & Company until 1859. Enoch Wedgwood became a partner in the pottery in c. 1856. Between c. 1856-1859, the firm used the mark "P.W. & W." for Podmore, Walker & Wedgwood. Enoch Wedgwood took over the older establishment in 1859 and changed the name to Wedgwood & Company.

The product of the firm was dinner and toilet sets in earthenware bodies hearlded as Pearl Stone Ware and Imperial Ironstone China. The wares were brightly painted, sponged, or decorated with transfer prints. Flow Blue patterns produced by Podmore, Walker & Company included California, Geraneum, Manilla, The Temple and Scinde.

MANILLA teapot and sugar with lion handles by Podmore, Walker & Company, circa 1845. The teapot measures 9" high and the sugar 7 1/2" high. *Courtesy of Dorothy & Elmer Caskey, Trojan Antiques, Cynthiana, Kentucky 41031.*

CALIFORNIA by Podmore, Walker & Company. The "& Company" was Enoch Wedgwood, making things complex as explained in the mark below. The date of registry was 1849. Impressed "PEARL STONE WARE" as well. 9 3/4" in diameter. *Courtesy of Anne & Dave Middleton, Pot O' Gold Antiques.*

## Marks

Podmore, Walker & Company used the initials "P.W. & CO." on several printed and impressed marks from 1834-1859 and frequently included the pattern names. The initials "P.W. & W." were employed from c. 1856-1859 when Enoch Wedgwood joined the firm.[28]

Podmore Walker & Company, Tunstall, Staffordshire, impressed P.W. & Co. manufacturers' mark used from 1834-1859 and impressed Pearl Stone Ware body type. *Courtesy of Louise and Charles Loehr, Louise's Old Things, Kutztown, Pennsylvania.*

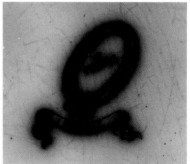

Podmore Walker & Company, Tunstall, Staffordshire, printed P.W. & Co. manufacturers' marks in use from 1834-1859. *Courtesy of Dorothy & Elmer Caskey, Trojan Antiques, Cynthiana, Kentucky 41031; Courtesy of Anne & Dave Middleton, Pot O' Gold Antiques.*

Podmore Walker & Company, Tunstall, Staffordshire, printed mark registered to Podmore, Walker & Company in 1849. The "& Co." in this case was Enoch Wedgwood and the owners found it to their advantage only to use the Wedgwood name in this case. From circa 1860 the firm was re-titled "Wedgwood & Co."[29] *Courtesy of Anne & Dave Middleton, Pot O' Gold Antiques.*

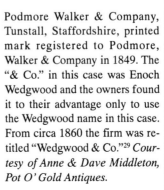

## The Ridgway Family

"J. Ridgway & Company is one of the most important manufacturers of earthenware in the Staffordshire potteries, and exhibits articles in this department of first-rate quality." — Juried Results of the Great International Exhibition of 1851.

The Ridgway family were Staffordshire potters primarily associated with two Hanley potteries, the Bell Works (1792) and Cauldon Place (1802). Two brothers, Job and George Ridgway, formed a partnership until Job Ridgway built Cauldon Works. Job was joined by his sons John and William Ridgway from 1814 to 1830. After 1830, until c. 1855 John directed the Cauldon Place Works while William ran the Bell Works. Cauldon Place Works would pass into the hands of Brown-Westhead, Moore & Company in 1862 and then to Cauldon Ltd. in 1905.

The Ridgway potteries produced useful wares of high workmanship in earthenwares, stonewares, and porcelain. Tea and dessert sets were specialities of the Ridgways. After 1830, William Ridgway manufactured finely molded jugs, stonewares, teapots, and candlesticks as well as delicate and finely decorated porcelain-styled tinted earthenware and stone china.

The Cauldon Place Works ceramics were described by Jewitt as, "... embrac[ing] almost every description of ceramic. In earthenware, all the usual table and toilet services and useful and ornamental articles of every class are made."

The Ridgways competed in and won medals for their exhibits at the major international exhibitions, including the Philadephia Centennial Exhibiton of 1876. William Ridgeway produced Flow Blue patterns which included Formosa and Penang (1830-1834). During the later years of the nineteenth and the early years of the twentieth centuries (1879-1920), Ridgways — the Bedford Works in Hanley —produced, among others, patterns christened Hong Kong, Kendal, Oriental, Osborne, Pagoda, and Peking in Flow Blue.

## Marks

The Ridgeway family used a number of printed and impressed marks of varying designs. One regular feature was the presence of the family name or initials in the marks. Pattern names were frequently included.

From c. 1830-1854, William Ridgway used his name "W. RIDGWAY" or initials with a variety of mark designs. In c. 1841 his son joined him and the name became "W. RIDGWAY, SON & CO." on the marks.

"RIDGWAYS" appears on the ceramics produced at the Bedford Works in Hanley from 1879 to 1920. A quiver and bow trade-mark was registered to the company in 1880. The company also reissued former marks with the initials "J&WR" and "W.R." after 1891 featuring a shield and flowers in one mark and an urn and beehive in the other.[30]

Ridgways, Shelton, Hanley, Staffordshire, printed stylized bow and quiver RIDGWAYS manufacturers' mark in use in circa 1912+ and KENDAL pattern name. *Courtesy of Louise and Charles Loehr, Louise's Old Things, Kutztown, Pennsylvania.*

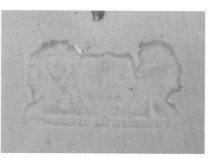

William Ridgway & Company, Bell Works, Shelton and Church Works, Hanley, Staffordshire, impressed W. R. & CO. manufacturers' mark with OPAQUE GRANITE CHINA body type, 1834-1854. *Courtesy of Lucille and Norman Bagdon.*

William Ridgway & Company, Bell Works, Shelton and Church Works, Hanley, Staffordshire, impressed W. R. & CO. manufacturers' mark with OPAQUE GRANITE CHINA body type, 1834-1854. *Courtesy of Joseph Nigro & Ralph Wick, Old Things Made New Again.*

William Ridgway Sons & Company, Church Works, Hanley, Staffordshire, printed W. R. S. & CO. manufacturers' mark including the HONG KONG pattern name, overlapping the previous W. R. & CO. impressed mark. This mark was in use from circa 1838-1848. *Courtesy of Dorothy & Arnold Kowalsky.*

OSBORNE plate by Ridgways, circa 1905. 9 3/4" in diameter. *Courtesy of Louise and Charles Loehr, Louise's Old Things, Kutztown, Pennsylvania.*

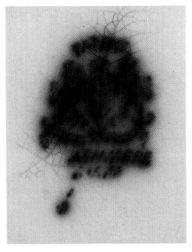

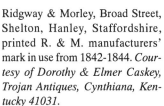

Ridgway & Morley, Broad Street, Shelton, Hanley, Staffordshire, printed R. & M. manufacturers' mark in use from 1842-1844. *Courtesy of Dorothy & Elmer Caskey, Trojan Antiques, Cynthiana, Kentucky 41031.*

Ridgways, Bedford Works, Hanley, Staffordshire, printed crown and circle mark with manufacturers' name beneath the crown, Royal Semi-Porcelain in the lower half of the circle, and OSBORNE pattern name below the circle. This mark was in use from circa 1905 to 1920. *Courtesy of Louise and Charles Loehr, Louise's Old Things, Kutztown, Pennsylvania.*

Ridgways, Bedford Works, Hanley, Staffordshire, printed urn and beehive manufacturers' mark with W. R. initials and England. This was a reissued mark in use after 1891. *Courtesy of Dorothy & Arnold Kowalsky.*

Clement Francis and Lawrence into partnership between 1859 and 1865. This brings us well into the period of Flow Blue production.

Of the earthenware produced by Wedgwood, Jewitt reports, "The goods produced are higher classes of earthenware, in which dinner, tea, breakfast, dessert, toilet and other services, and all the usual miscellaneous articles, are made to a very considerable extent, both for the home, colonial, Continental, and American markets, to which considerable quantities are regularly exported." The company's "Imperial Ironstone China" was considered to be the staple of the firm. The quality was considered to be excellent and the decoration admirable. When exhibited at international exhibitions, Wedgwood ceramics received positive attention.

By the middle of the nineteenth century, tablewares were mainly transfer printed. A variety of all covering patterns were based on chinoiserie views, floral studies and other designs popular during the period. Of the transfer printed patterns, one considered the most successful during the latter half of the nineteenth century was "Asiatic Pheasants."

Wedgwood's "Best patterns" were influenced by oriental styles and were decorated with prunus blossoms, insects, bamboo leaves, birds and angular patterns around the rim. These were initially flowing patterns. They may have first been offered at high prices too, if the firm followed the philosophy of it's founder Josiah Wedgwood. Josiah Wedgwood I believed that quality goods must first be offered at high prices "...to make the[m] esteemed 'Ornaments for Palaces'..." Patterns produced in Flow Blue by Wedgwood included Chapoo, Chinese, Chusan, Hollyhock, Ivanhoe, Rose and Jasmine.

## The Wedgwood Family

"The aim of the firm is, and always has been, to produce the best, most artistic, and most pleasingly effective designs, and to adapt them to ordinary purposes, so that they may become the everyday surroundings of the artisan as well as of the educated man of taste." — Llewellynn Jewitt, 1877

Josiah Wedgwood I (1730-1795) established the pottery in Burslem in 1759 and it was controlled by the family until becoming a public company in 1967. Briefly, Josaiah Wedgwood I son, Josiah Wedgwood II was succeeded at the time of his death in 1841 by his sons Joshiah III and Francis. Joshiah III became a partner in 1823 and remained so until his retirement in 1842. Francis joined the firm as a partner in 1827 and controlled the company from 1842 to 1870. Francis went into a brief partnership with J. Boyle and Robert Brown. He took his sons Godfrey,

CHUSAN drainer by Wedgewood, circa. 1882. 103/4" x 8 1/2". *Courtesy of Dorothy & Arnold Kowalsky.*

## Marks

The Wedgwood custom was to meticulously mark their wares; these were Wedgwood products and they wanted their customers to know it. Nearly all their ceramics bear the impressed "WEDGWOOD" mark. "ENGLAND" was added in 1892 and "MADE IN ENGLAND" in 1911. Pattern names frequently appear. Various impressed and printed marks in a wide range of designs have been used over the years with the Wedgwood name, changing with time and association between several potting factories the family maintained.

Wedgwood also employed a three letter code in which the third letter represented the year beginning in 1860. Variations to this standard formula begin in 1907.[31]

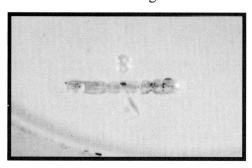

Josiah Wedgwood (& Sons Ltd.), Burslem, Etruria, and Barlaston, Staffordshire, the impressed upper case WEDGWOOD mark was in use from 1769 to the present. From 1860 onward a three-letter dating system was employed, the third letter indicating the year of production. *Courtesy of Dorothy & Arnold Kowalsky.*

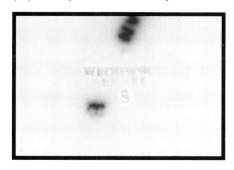

Josiah Wedgwood (& Sons Ltd.), Burslem, Etruria, and Barlaston, Staffordshire, impressed upper case WEDGWOOD mark with the addition of the name PEARL for Pearl body was produced from circa 1840-1868. After 1868 a simple P was used. *Courtesy of Dorothy & Arnold Kowalsky.*

Josiah Wedgwood (& Sons Ltd.), Burslem, Etruria, and Barlaston, Staffordshire, impressed upper case WEDGWOOD mark with the addition of the name ETRURIA was used from circa 1840-1845. *Courtesy of Dorothy & Arnold Kowalsky.*

## American Manufacturers

"One article is shown from America." — Juried Results of the Great International Exhibition of 1851.[32]

No comment was made by the jury in 1851 as to the quality of the American ware on display or even to the name of the firm presenting it. This summed up the feeling abroad and in America as to the quality or importance of American ceramics.

The reticence of American consumers to purchase American pottery, and the lack of regard for their wares both at home and abroad, drove the American potting community to vow in 1875 to produce original wares which could compare favorably to, and compete against, foreign competition. American potters seized the opportunity presented by the Philadelphia Centennial Exhibition of 1876 to improve their image. They did not miss their chance, displaying a variety of impressive and competitive wares. The fortune of American potteries improved during the last quarter of the nineteenth century.[33]

While the total number of American firms choosing to compete with England in Flow Blue was not large, here are notable American potters who produced Flow Blue in an attempt to capture part of that market from their British rivals. (see Snyder, *Flow Blue. A Collectors Guide to Pattern, History and Values.* for examples of several of these companies' works and manufacturers' marks.)

### Burgess & Campbell, International Pottery Company

The International Pottery Company works were established in 1860 by Henry Speeler in Trenton, New Jersey. Trenton was a popular potting town, supporting nineteen potteries in 1875, producing varied ceramic forms worth roughly two million dollars. With easy access to clays and transportation upon the Delaware and Chesapeake canal systems and docking sites along the Delaware River, Trenton was dubbed "the Staffordshire of America" during the last quarter of the nineteenth century.

Henry Speeler brought his two sons into the firm in 1868, admitting them into partnership under the name to Henry Speeler & Sons. The pottery was purchased by Carr and Clark, with assistance from James and John Moses and renamed Lincoln Pottery. Later, in 1879 Burgess and Campbell purchased the works, trading under the Burgess & Campbell name. In 1903, Campbell left the firm. The pottery was renamed again, this time as Burgess and Company.

Burgess & Campbell produced semi-porcelain, toilet wares and hotel ware. They produced "Royal Blue" and "Rugby Flint" wares as well. Porcelain was produced with marginal success until 1888 when a high-quality body paste was introduced. The firm specialized in dinner and toilet sets with elegant forms in semi-porcelain. These were decorated with underglazed grey, dark or lighter blues.

A portion of their semi-porcelain production of blue underglazed transfer printed wares were flown. Royal Blue was produced in Flow Blue. Of Royal Blue, Edwin Barber stated that on their "Wilton" china Burgess & Campbell produced, "...the same pattern as the 'Royal Blue,' decorated in 'still blue' and gray underglaze." Using a Maltese Cross manufacturers' mark including the pottery monogram "IPC" for the International Pottery Company, either Burgess and Campell or Burgess and Company also produced a "Cracked Ice" pattern in Flow Blue.

ROYAL BLUE platter by Burgess & Campbell, circa 1880. 12 5/8" x 8 1/4". *Courtesy of Dorothy & Arnold Kowalsky.*

## Marks

Burgess and Campbell produced a number of printed marks with the full name "Burgess & Campbell" or the initials "B & C" printed on each mark. They produced circular marks with pattern names printed in the center and the company name within the circle. They also produced a printed double shield mark that Carr and Clark had used previously.[34]

## Colonial Pottery Company

The Colonial Pottery Company operated in East Liverpool, Ohio from 1903 to 1929. The pottery produced ironstone and semi-porcelain. Their semi-porcelain was heavy, considered to have a nice white body, decorated with transfer printed designs and much gold trim.

## Marks

The Colonial Pottery Company produced a variety of printed manufacturers' marks including the name "The Colonial Co.". Several marks contained an eagle's head and the body type name.[35]

## The French China Company

The French China Company was founded shortly before 1900 in Sebring, Ohio and remained in business as an independent pottery until 1916. In 1916, the company joined the Sebring Manufacturing Company with the Saxon China Company and the Strong Manufacturing Company. While these were consolidated under one management, each plant retained its original name. In 1929, the Sebring Manufacturing Corporation joined American Chinaware Corporation, which failed in 1931. Following this failure, American Chinaware Corporation dissolved and the French China and Saxon China companies both closed their doors in 1932. It should be noted, however, that in c. 1934 the Saxon China Company reopened as the French-Saxon China Company.

The French China Company produced table and toilet wares in both semi-porcelain and white granite bodies. According to Barber, the pottery produced wares with pattern and shape names including: "Lygia" dinner wares, the "Cupid" toilet pattern, "Greek" and "Tiger" toilet services, and "Kenneth" and "Pluto" toilet sets. The pottery produced Flow Blue marked "La Francaise Porcelain."

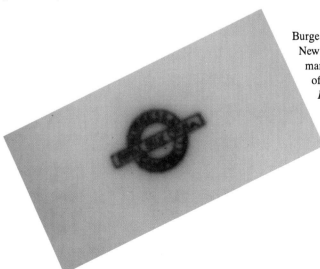

Burgess & Campbell, International Pottery Company, Trenton, New Jersey, printed BURGESS & CAMPBELL manufacturers' mark including the name ROYAL BLUE CHINA. The period of use for this mark is indeterminate at this time. *Courtesy of Dorothy & Arnold Kowalsky.*

USS BROOKLYN bowl by The French China Company, circa 1900-1916. 10 3/4" in diameter. *Courtesy of Dorothy & Elmer Caskey, Trojan Antiques, Cynthiana, Kentucky 41031.*

## Marks

The French China Company produced printed manufacturers' marks. Some were the names of patterns or ware types alone while others included the full "French China Co." name or "F.C. Co." initials. Body ware types such as semi-vitreous were included at times as was a "La Francaise Porcelain" mark.[36]

The French China Company, Sebring, Ohio, printed LA FRANCAISE PORCELAIN manufacturers' mark in use from circa 1900-1916. *Courtesy of Dorothy & Elmer Caskey, Trojan Antiques, Cynthiana, Kentucky 41031.*

## Mayer China Company

In 1880, Joseph and Arthur Mayer arrived in New York from England. By 1881 they had moved to Beaver County, Pennsylvania and established the J & E Mayer Potteries Company, Ltd along the banks of Beaver Falls. The pottery works were later incorporated as the Mayer China Company. The company continues throughout the twentieth century to date.

Prior to c. 1914-1915 when the pottery concentrated solely on hotel wares, Mayer China Company produced a wide variety of ceramic wares in white granite ware and semi-vitreous china. Table, toilet and odd sets of wares, both plain and with underglazed transfer prints, were produced. By 1901, the company employed 145 individuals to produce white granite alone. By 1915, only twenty-five percent of Mayer China Company's product was decorated. Plain white wares were on the rise.

Shapes christened Amazon and Nile were produced in toilet wares. Pattern names included Columbia, Duquesne, and prior to an 1896 fire, on special services appeared Diana, Potomac, and Windsor patterns. In Flow Blue an Argyle pattern was included.

USS MAINE bowl by The French China Company, circa 1900-1916. 9 1/2" x 12 3/4". *Courtesy of Dorothy & Elmer Caskey, Trojan Antiques, Cynthiana, Kentucky 41031.*

## Marks

Mayer China Company produced a wide variety of printed marks. The common feature was the presence of the company name: first "J. & E. Mayer" and later "Mayer China." Pattern and shape names were included at times as well as the body type.[37]

## Mercer Pottery Company

Mercer Pottery Company was organized in Trenton, New Jersey in 1868 by James Moses. The pottery produced wares with ironstone or white granite, semi-vitreous and semi-porcelain bodies. Moses claimed to be the first potter in the United States to produce semi-porcelain wares, which he christened "Parisian Granite."

Among the ware types the company produced were dinner and toilet sets, druggist supplies, and sanitary wares. The Mercer Pottery Company continued production into the mid-1930s. The pottery was no longer listed among Trenton's many potteries in 1937. However, a second factory, Mercer Porcelain carried on for another year, closing in 1938.

Barber states that the shapes used by both Mercer Pottery and International Pottery companies were virtually interchangable with only the name below the manufacturers' mark changed.

Mercer Pottery Company produced underglazed blue transfer printed designs. Among their Flow Blue patterns were Luzerne and Paisley.

## Marks

Mercer Pottery Company produced many printed marks featuring either the full company name or some part of the name: "Mercer Pottery Co.", "Mercer Pottery", and simply "Mercer". At times the name of the body type is included as is the pattern name.

Barber comments on a double shield mark used by the company prior to the turn of the century. This mark was employed by Carr & Clark and Burgess & Campbell in Trenton as well as by James Carr at the New York City Pottery. It was created by Carr & Clark when they reorganized the International Pottery Company works. They had been assisted by James and John Moses. Clark was English and James Moses American and as such they saw the double shield as appropriate. When Burgess & Campbell bought out Carr & Clark, they too continued to use the double shield mark.

Frequently found on Flow Blue is a "Mercer" manufacturers' mark featuring a single shield, a crown and a draped cloak surrounding the shield.[38]

## Sebring Pottery Company

The Sebring Pottery works were first established in 1887 in East Liverpool, Ohio. The company moved to Sebring, Ohio after the town was founded in 1898. The pottery works survived the Depression and continued operations into the 1940s. At that time, Sebring Pottery Company was purchased by Limoges and some of their line continued.

This pottery produced semi-porcelains. In 1923 the company introduced their "Ivory Porcelain" ware at an exhibition in Pittsburgh. Flow Blue patterns produced by Sebring Pottery include a Delph pattern.

## Marks

A wide variety of printed manufacturers' marks were produced. The full name "Sebring Pottery Co." or some portion of it was employed regularly in the marks. As of 1923 an "Ivory Porcelain" body ware mark appeared as a back mark. Many of the marks were also outlined in the shape of the state of Ohio. Pattern names were included at times.[39]

## Warwick China Company

Warwick China Company of Wheeling, West Virginia began production in 1884, was incorporated in 1887, and would not close it's doors for the last time until 1957. Warwick was recognised for their production of beautiful dinner sets of high quality porcelain. They also manufactured semi-porcelains and hotel wares. At their height, Warwick China manufactured over 10,000 dinnerware sets a month.

Warwick used hand painting, transfer prints (some of which were flown), tin types, and decals over the years. While Warwick China Company did not name their patterns, they had hundreds at their command. However, Warwick did name their body shapes, which included Avon, Colonial, Sheraton, Regency and Warwick.

A marble pattern syrup with a hinged silver lid by the Warwick China Company, circa 1893. 3 3/4" high to spout. *Courtesy of Joseph Nigro & Ralph Wick, Old Things Made New Again.*

## Marks

Warwick China Company used a range of printed manufacturers' marks. The first featured a helmet and crossed swords. This would continue to be used for an extended period and was registered on July 12, 1905. The name "Warwick" or "Warwick China" was a regular feature of their marks. The company also used the initials "IOGA" with their mark on some of the finest of their early wares including Flow Blue, tankard pitchers, plates, vases, and umbrella holders.

From 1893 to 1898, the company used a "Warwick Semi-Porcelain" mark. After 1912, Warwick produced hotel wares and after 1940 included offered some bone china. During their last few years, hotel ware would be their mainstay.[40]

Warwack China Company, Wheeling, West Virginia, printed manufacturers' mark in use from 1893 to 1898. *Courtesy of Joseph Nigro & Ralph Wick, Old Things Made New Again.*

## Wheeling Pottery Company

Wheeling Pottery Company was established in Wheeling, West Virginia in November of 1879 with five kilns and 150 men. In 1882, Charles Craddock — a Staffordshire artist formerly employed by Mintons Ltd. — was hired and would become the head of the decorating department. In 1887, La Belle Pottery Company was created under the same management to produce "Adamantine" china from 1888 to 1893. In 1889 the two companies were consolidated. On January 1, 1903, Wheeling Pottery Company was organized, combining Wheeling, La Belle, Riverside and Avon potteries as departments within the company. This combined organization produced sanitary wares, utilitarian pottery, semi-porcelains and artwares. The firm went into receivership in 1910 and was reorganized as the Wheeling Sanitary Manufacturing Company.

Wheeling Pottery Company originally produced white granite wares or "Queensware." It would be three or four years before "Queensware" was decorated. After Wheeling and La Belle combined, a thin and artistically designed "Cameo" china was produced. By 1904, the company employed roughly 1,200 individuals, manufacturing everything from basic sanitary wares to fine china. At that time, this combined facility was one of the largest employers of it's type in the nation.

Flow Blue wares were produced at the Wheeling factory, along with complete lines of dinnerware, tankards, "Virginia Girl" plates, cracker jars, jardinieres, and children's products. One of the firms semi-porcelain lines was christened "La Belle" china. Referring to the china body itself rather than the pattern, this mark is often found in Flow Blue in association with Wheeling Pottery. While "La Belle" may be found with decorations of varying themes, collectors and dealers alike have used the "La Belle" name in association with a specific floral pattern produced by the Wheeling Pottery Company.

"La Belle" pattern syrup with a hinged silver lid by the Wheeling Pottery Company, Wheeling, West Virginia, dating from circa 1893. 4 1/4" high. *Courtesy of Joseph Nigro & Ralph Wick, Old Things Made New Again.*

"La Belle" jardiniere stand by Wheeling Pottery Company, dating from circa 1894. 15 3/4" high. *Courtesy of Dorothy & Elmer Caskey, Trojan Antiques, Cynthiana, Kentucky 41031.*

"La Belle" pitcher by Wheeling Pottery Company, dating from circa 1893. 7 3/8" high to the spout. From the tip of spout to the end of the handle the pitcher measures 8 1/4". *Courtesy of Dorothy & Arnold Kowalsky.*

## Marks

Wheeling Pottery Company employed a wide range of marks featuring the full name or the "W.P.C." initials of the firm. Among their marks was a center circle with an eagle below, six flags along the sides, "WARRENTED" above, and "MADE IN AMERICA" below. Another circular mark featured a globe, eagle with shield, and a banner reading "STONE CHINA". A mark with a decidedly English appearance featured a lion and unicorn with "ROYAL IRONSTONE CHINA" printed above.[41]

Wheeling Pottery Company, Wheeling, West Virginia, printed LA BELLE CHINA manufacturers' mark in use from 1893 to 1910. *Courtesy of Joseph Nigro & Ralph Wick, Old Things Made New Again.*

Wheeling Pottery Company, Wheeling, West Virginia, printed W. P. LA BELLE CHINA manufacturers' mark in use from 1893 to 1910. *Courtesy of Dorothy & Elmer Caskey, Trojan Antiques, Cynthiana, Kentucky 41031.*

## European Manufacturers

Several of the potteries on the Continent took up Flow Blue manufacture during the later decades of the nineteenth century. Their efforts were largely directed toward the export market.

## Keller & Guérin

The French firm of Keller & Guérin produced a limited amount of Flow Blue from the historic Luneville pottery works. Located in the contested province of Lorraine which was not ceded to Germany following the Franco-Prussian War (1870-1871), the Luneville works had been established in 1731. In Flow Blue, the firm produced patterns including "Luneville Blue." Keller & Guérin ceased their operation in 1914.

LUNEVILLE BLUE sauce ladle by Keller & Guérin, circa 1891. *Courtesy of Dorothy & Arnold Kowalsky.*

## Marks

Keller & Guérin's manufacturers' mark included the initials "KG" and the "LUNEVILLE" company name. In Flow Blue, the marks found date predominantly from 1880 through the 1890s.[42]

## Utzschneider & Company

Paul Utzschneider established his large firm in the clay rich Sarreguemines, Lorraine in France in 1770. The pottery continued to be run by the Utzschneider family into the early twentieth century. The firm continues in production of porcelains and faience.

Prior to the middle of the nineteenth century, the pottery's principal production was faience. However, in the 1860s the company increased the range of their output into other ware types, including — in time — Flow Blue in patterns such as Persian Moss and some hand-painted designs. The quality of their product was consistently high. Inspiration for Utzschneider & Company's designs was often taken from English patterns.

Following the triumph of Bismarck in the Franco-Prussian War, with the annexation of a portion of Lorraine, Utzschneider & Company expanded their works to maintain French status. The pottery became the largest of its kind in France, employing over 2,000 workers.

## Marks

The common denominator in the Utzschneider & Company manufacturers' marks, whether impressed or printed, are the initials "U & C" or simply "U C" and the name "Sarreguemines."[43]

## Villeroy & Boch

Among the principal German potters, Villeroy & Boch was established in 1836 when the company founded in 1748 by Francois Boch merged with the Villeroy family works, creating one of the largest manufacturers in Europe. The firm continues in production.

Villeroy & Boch was concentrated in Mettlach in the Rhineland between c. 1860 and 1900. Vast quantities of Villeroy and Boch ceramics, predominantly earthenwares, were destined for American shores. Among their Flow Blue were a Fasan and an India pattern.

## Marks

Villeroy & Boch is assiduous in marking their wares. The most common mark is an impressed or printed roundel including the letters "VBM" for Villeroy & Boch, Mettlach.[44]

Villeroy & Boch, Mettlach, Germany, printed V & B manufacturers' mark including the INDIA pattern name, dating from circa 1890. *Courtesy of Louise and Charles Loehr, Louise's Old Things, Kutztown, Pennsylvania.*

INDIA Teapot without lid by Villeroy & Boch, circa 1890. 6 1/2" H. without lid. *Courtesy of Louise and Charles Loehr, Louise's Old Things, Kutztown, Pennsylvania.*

## The Early Victorian Period: 1835 to 1860

During the Early Victorian period, Chinoiseries, the Romantic Movement, and the stirrings of a fascination with the natural world influenced Flow Blue designs.

Meanwhile, in 1835 Francis II, the last Holy Roman Emperor and Emperor of Austria died. Phineas Taylor Barnum — American showman extraordinary — began his career in that year by exhibiting Joyce Heth, an elderly African-American woman Barnum claimed was the nurse of George Washington, making her over 160 years old! Texas won independence from Mexico, becoming a republic with General Sam Houston as it's first president while Asa Gray gave the world the first botanical textbook "Elements of Botony" in 1836. Victoria (1819-1901) became Queen of Great Britian in 1837. An American army officer, Abner Doubleday, laid out the first field in Cooperstown, New York and played the first baseball game ever in 1839.[1]

By the end of the period, Richard Burton and John Speke had discovered Lake Tanganyika and Lake Victoria Nyanza in 1858. In 1859, Oregon became a state and Charles Darwin released "On the Origins of Species by Natural Selection." Finally, in 1860 Abraham Lincoln was elected the 16th President of the United State. South Carolina seceded in protest.[2]

ACADIA soup tureen underplate by Hackwood, circa 1827-1855. 14 1/2" x 12". *Courtesy of Joseph Nigro & Ralph Wick, Old Things Made New Again.*

ACADIA pitcher by one of several Hackwoods located in Shelton and Hanley from 1827 to 1855. 8 1/4" high. *Courtesy of Joseph Nigro & Ralph Wick, Old Things Made New Again.*

Hackwood printed manufacturers' mark including the initial "H" and the "ACADIA" pattern name. The Hackwood's were William Hackwood, Hanley (1827-1843), Josiah Hackwood, Hanley (1842-1843), William & Thomas Hackwood, Shelton (1844-1850), and Thomas Hackwood (1850-1855).[7] *Courtesy of Joseph Nigro & Ralph Wick, Old Things Made New Again.*

AMOY teapot by Davenport, 1844. 9 1/2" high. *Courtesy of Louise and Charles Loehr, Louise's Old Things, Kutztown, Pennsylvania.*

AMOY teapot, sugar, creamer, and waste bowl by Davenport, 1848. The teapot measures 10" high, the waste bowl 5 3/4" in diameter and 3 1/2" high, and the creamer measures 5" high to the spout. *Courtesy of Joseph Nigro & Ralph Wick, Old Things Made New Again.*

AMOY pitchers by Davenport, 1848. The pitchers measure 9", 8", and 5 3/4" high to the spout. *Courtesy of Joseph Nigro & Ralph Wick, Old Things Made New Again.*

Two AMOY cup plates and a child's platter by Davenport. The child's platter dated to 1848. *Courtesy of Joseph Nigro & Ralph Wick, Old Things Made New Again.*

Two AMOY cup plates with partial designs on each. These were manufactured by Davenport and stamped with an 1848 date. 4 1/8" diameter. *Courtesy of Dorothy & Arnold Kowalsky.*

BAMBOO Platter by Samuel Alcock & Company, circa 1845. 16 3/4" x 13 7/8". *Courtesy of Louise and Charles Loehr, Louise's Old Things, Kutztown, Pennsylvania.*

AMOY open vegetable by Davenport, circa 1848. 13 1/2" x 10 1/4". *Courtesy of Joseph Nigro & Ralph Wick, Old Things Made New Again.*

BAMBOO under and over glazed platter by Thomas Dimmock, circa 1845. 21 1/2" x 17 1/4". *Courtesy of Dorothy & Arnold Kowalsky.*

BERRY hot water plate by William Ridgway, circa 1840. Hot water plates are usually produced with metal bases. 10 1/4" in diameter. 2 3/8" high. *Courtesy of Dorothy & Arnold Kowalsky.*

BIMRAH covered vegetable dish by Flacket, Toft & Robinson, Church Street, Longton, Staffordshire, produced from 1857-58 with the printed initial manufacturers' mark F. T. & R., Godden mark 1569. This covered vegetable dish measures 12 1/4" x 10 1/2" across the handles and 8" in height. *Courtesy of Dorothy & Arnold Kowalsky.*

BLACKBERRY platter by Francis Morley & Company, 1845-58. 21 1/2" wide. *Courtesy of Lucille and Norman Bagdon.*

Francis Morley (& Company), Shelton, Hanley, Staffordshire, printed "F. M. & CO." manufacturers' mark with "BLACKBERRY" pattern name, in use from 1845-1858. *Courtesy of Lucille and Norman Bagdon.*

BLUE BELL sauce tureen with underplate and ladle by William Ridgway & Company, 1834-54. Note the rose bud finial. The tureen measures 7" high, 5 3/4" in diameter; the underplate measures 7 1/2" in length; the ladle measures 6 3/4" in length. *Courtesy of Dorothy & Elmer Caskey, Trojan Antiques, Cynthiana, Kentucky 41031.*

BLACKBERRY Lustre Coffee pot in the grand loop style by Mellor, Venables & Company, Burslem, Staffordshire (1834-1851). 11" high. *Courtesy of Dorothy & Arnold Kowalsky.*

BLUE BELL covered vegetable by William Ridgway & Company, 1834-54. 12" x 10 1/4" x 6" high. *Courtesy of Lucille and Norman Bagdon.*

BLUE BELL tray by William Ridgway & Company, 1834-54, with an impressed "OPAQUE GRANITE CHINA" body type mark. *Courtesy of Joseph Nigro & Ralph Wick, Old Things Made New Again.*

BLUE BELL syrup by Dillwyn, Swansea, Wales, 1840. *Courtesy of Lucille and Norman Bagdon.*

CABUL eight-sided full panel gothic teapot by Edward Challinor. The pattern was registered in 1847. 8" high. *Courtesy of Lucille and Norman Bagdon.*

CARLTON platter by Samuel Alcock & Company, circa 1850. 15 3/4" x 12 1/4". *Courtesy of Louise and Charles Loehr, Louise's Old Things, Kutztown, Pennsylvania.*

CHINESE well and tree platter by Thomas Dimmock, circa 1845. 15 1/2". *Courtesy of Lucille and Norman Bagdon.*

CHINESE polychrome sponge dish by Thomas Dimmock, circa 1845. *Courtesy of Lucille and Norman Bagdon.*

CHINESE polychrome vase by Thomas Dimmock, circa 1845. *Courtesy of Lucille and Norman Bagdon.*

CHING platter by Davenport with a manufacturers' mark used from 1820 to 1860. 15 3/4" x 12". *Courtesy of Dorothy & Arnold Kowalsky.*

CHUSAN fruit bowl by Joseph Clementson, circa 1835. 12 1/4" diameter x 4 1/2" high. *Courtesy of Anne & Dave Middleton, Pot O' Gold Antiques.*

CHUSAN platter by Joseph Clementson, circa 1835. 16". *Courtesy of Lucille and Norman Bagdon.*

CHUSAN sauce tureen and underplate by Joseph Clementson, circa 1835. The underplate measures 9" x 6 1/4", and the tureen 8" x 4" x 6 1/4" high. *Courtesy of Joseph Nigro & Ralph Wick, Old Things Made New Again.*

CHUSAN, small bowl by Peter Holdcroft & Company, 1846-1852. 6" in diameter. *Courtesy of Dorothy & Arnold Kowalsky.*

CHUSAN jam dish with lid by Joseph Clementson, circa 1835. 5 1/2" dia, 4 1/2" high. *Courtesy of Joseph Nigro & Ralph Wick, Old Things Made New Again.*

Peter Holdcroft & Company, Lower Works, Fountain Place, Burslem, printed "P. H. & CO." manufacturers' mark in use from 1846 to 1852. *Courtesy of Dorothy & Arnold Kowalsky.*

DAHLIA covered vegetable dish by Edward Challinor, circa 1850. 7" high and 10 3/4" in diameter. *Courtesy of Louise and Charles Loehr, Louise's Old Things, Kutztown, Pennsylvania.*

FORMOSA platter by Thomas, John & Joseph Mayer, circa 1850. 15 1/2". *Courtesy of Lucille and Norman Bagdon.*

DEJAPORE vase by George Phillips. Longport, 1834-48. The registration mark indicates an 1846 registration date. 11 1/2" high. *Courtesy of Joseph Nigro & Ralph Wick, Old Things Made New Again.*

George Phillips. Longport, Staffordshire, printed "G. PHILLIPS" manufacturers' mark with a "DEJAPORE" pattern name. The registration mark indicates an 1846 registration date. *Courtesy of Joseph Nigro & Ralph Wick, Old Things Made New Again.*

FORMOSA plate by Thomas, John & Joseph Mayer, circa 1850. 7 3/8" in diameter. *Courtesy of Louise and Charles Loehr, Louise's Old Things, Kutztown, Pennsylvania.*

"The Fisherman" teacup and saucer by Podmore, Walker, & Company, 1834-1859. The cup measures 3 3/4" in diameter and 3" high; the saucer measures 5 7/8" in diameter. *Courtesy of Joseph Nigro & Ralph Wick, Old Things Made New Again.*

FORMOSA creamer, teapot, and sugar by
Thomas, John & Joseph Mayer, circa 1850.
*Courtesy of Lucille and Norman Bagdon.*

FORMOSA twelve panel chocolate cup by
Thomas, John & Joseph Mayer, circa 1850.
Height: 3 1/2". *Courtesy of Dorothy & Arnold
Kowalsky.*

GOTHA plate by Joseph Heath, 1845-1853. 4 1/4" in diameter. *Courtesy of Dorothy & Arnold Kowalsky.*

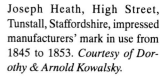

Joseph Heath, High Street,
Tunstall, Staffordshire, impressed
manufacturers' mark in use from
1845 to 1853. *Courtesy of Dorothy & Arnold Kowalsky.*

"Heart with Arrow" (authors designation) Soup tureen by William Ridgway & Company, produced prior to 1845. 10 1/2" high; handle to handle 14" in length; 11" in diameter. *Courtesy of Dorothy & Arnold Kowalsky.*

HONG vase by Anthony Shaw, circa 1855. 11 3/4" high x 8 1/4" diameter *Courtesy of Joseph Nigro & Ralph Wick, Old Things Made New Again.*

Anthony Shaw (& Co.)(& Son), Tunstall (circa 1851-1856); Burslem (circa 1860-circa 1900). The full name or "A. Shaw" was found among several printed or impressed marks from 1851-1882. The "HONG" pattern name is included. In circa 1882, "& SON" was added to the mark until circa 1898. Replacing "& SON" in circa 1898 was "& CO." and was in use until circa 1900 when the firm was purchased by A.J. Wilkinson Ltd. *Courtesy of Joseph Nigro & Ralph Wick, Old Things Made New Again.*

HONG platter by Petrus Regout, circa 1858. 17 1/2" x 13 7/8". *Courtesy of Dorothy & Arnold Kowalsky.*

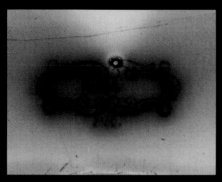

Petrus Regout, Maastricht, Holland, in business from 1836-1931+, printed and impressed manufacturers' marks. Printed "P.R." manufacturers' initials and "HONG" pattern name; impressed "REGOUT" and "MAASTRICHT" marks. In use circa 1858. *Courtesy of Dorothy & Arnold Kowalsky.*

HYSON tray with unique custard background color by Samuel Alcock, 1845. 9" x 11". *Courtesy of Dorothy & Elmer Caskey, Trojan Antiques, Cynthiana, Kentucky 41031.*

HYSON pedestaled fruit bowl with unique custard background color by Samuel Alcock, 1845. 6 1/2" high, 10 1/2" in diameter. *Courtesy of Dorothy & Elmer Caskey, Trojan Antiques, Cynthiana, Kentucky 41031.*

INDIA pattern pedestalled dish by Villeroy & Boch, circa 1845. 12 1/4" x 8". *Courtesy of Dorothy & Arnold Kowalsky.*

INDIA coffee pot by Villeroy & Boch, circa 1845. 7 3/4" high. *Courtesy of Joseph Nigro & Ralph Wick, Old Things Made New Again.*

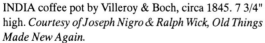

INDIAN STONE platter by Edward Walley, circa 1850. 20 1/4" x 15 3/4". *Courtesy of Joseph Nigro & Ralph Wick, Old Things Made New Again.*

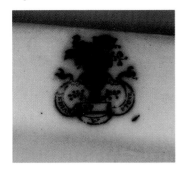

Edward Walley, Cobridge, Staffordshire, printed "W" initial mark with "INDIAN STONE" pattern name in use from 1845 to 1856. *Courtesy of Joseph Nigro & Ralph Wick, Old Things Made New Again.*

JEDDO platter by William Adams & Son, circa 1845. 18" in length. *Courtesy of Lucille and Norman Bagdon.*

INDIANAH cup and saucer, maker unknown, circa 1850. The cup measures 3 1/2" in diameter and the saucer 6" in diameter. *Courtesy of Joseph Nigro & Ralph Wick, Old Things Made New Again.*

IVY platter by Davenport, circa 1820-1860. 13" x 9 3/4". *Courtesy of Louise and Charles Loehr, Louise's Old Things, Kutztown, Pennsylvania.*

IVY pitcher by Thomas Dimmock, 1844. 7 1/4" high to the spout. *Courtesy of Lucille and Norman Bagdon.*

KAOLIN platter by Podmore, Walker & Company, clearly impressed "PEARL STONE WARE" (so Kaolin does not refer to the body of the ware), 1834-1859. 13 1/8" x 10 1/2". *Courtesy of Dorothy & Arnold Kowalsky.*

KIN SHAN platter by Edward Challinor, circa 1855. 16 1/2". *Courtesy of Lucille and Norman Bagdon.*

KIN SHAN soup ladle by Edward Challinor, circa 1855. The ladle bowl measures 3 3/4" in diameter and the ladle measures 8 3/4" long. *Courtesy of Lucille and Norman Bagdon.*

KIN SHAN coffee pot by Edward Challinor, circa 1855. 11 1/4" high. *Courtesy of Lucille and Norman Bagdon.*

KREMLIN tea cup and saucer and small plate by Samuel Alcock and Company, circa 1830-1859. *Courtesy of Dorothy & Elmer Caskey, Trojan Antiques, Cynthiana, Kentucky 41031.*

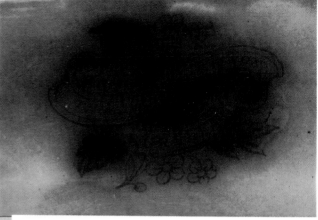

Thomas Phillips & Son, Furlong Pottery, Burslem, Staffordshire. Printed or impressed "THOS. PHILLIPS & SON" manufacturers' marks were used from circa 1845-1846. *Courtesy of Dorothy & Arnold Kowalsky.*

LA HORE by Thomas Phillips & Son, Furlong Pottery, Burslem, circa 1845-1846. 13 1/2" x 10 5/8". *Courtesy of Dorothy & Arnold Kowalsky.*

LAZULI candlesticks by Dillwyn, Swansea, Wales. This sheet pattern was used on toilet wares from 1836-1850. The name is short for lapis lazuli. 6 1/4" high, 4" base diameter. *Courtesy of Dorothy & Arnold Kowalsky.*

LAZULI paired set of candlesticks by Dillwyn, Swansea, Wales. 7 1/4" high, 4 1/4" base diameter. *Courtesy of Dorothy & Arnold Kowalsky.*

LILY well & tree platter by Thomas Dimmock, circa 1850. 21 1/4" x 16 1/4". *Courtesy of Joseph Nigro & Ralph Wick, Old Things Made New Again.*

LAZULI unpaired set of candlesticks by Dillwyn, Swansea, Wales. 8" high, 5 5/8" base diameter; 7" high, 5 1/2" base diameter. *Courtesy of Dorothy & Arnold Kowalsky.*

"Leaf and Swag" brushstroke razor box, unidentified manufacturer, circa 1850. 8" x 3". *Courtesy of Louise and Charles Loehr, Louise's Old Things, Kutztown, Pennsylvania.*

LINTIN egg cups by Thomas Godwin, Canal Works, Navigation Road, Burslem, Staffordshire. Thomas Godwin produced earthenwares from 1834-1854. Lintin is the name of an island in the Pearl River near Canton. 2 1/4" in diameter and in height. *Courtesy of Lucille and Norman Bagdon.*

LONSDALE soup tureen by Samuel Alcock & Company. This was ORIENTAL by an earlier firm and the quality of later period reproduction of the pattern was not nearly as good. The "S.A. & CO." mark on the base was in use from circa 1830-1859. 11" high, *Courtesy of Dorothy & Elmer Caskey, Trojan Antiques, Cynthiana, Kentucky 41031.*

LOZERN punch cup by Edward Challinor, circa 1850. *Courtesy of Joseph Nigro & Ralph Wick, Old Things Made New Again.*

MADRAS well & tree by Davenport, circa 1845. 19" x 14 7/8". *Courtesy of Dorothy & Arnold Kowalsky.*

MADRAS lavatory pan by Davenport, circa 1845. 12" in diameter. *Courtesy of Joseph Nigro & Ralph Wick, Old Things Made New Again.*

MANILLA platter by Podmore, Walker & Company, circa 1845. 13 1/4" x 10". *Courtesy of Dorothy & Elmer Caskey, Trojan Antiques, Cynthiana, Kentucky 41031.*

MANILLA butter bowls —table and individual— by Podmore, Walker & Company, circa 1845. 7" & 9 1/2" in diameter. *Courtesy of Dorothy & Elmer Caskey, Trojan Antiques, Cynthiana, Kentucky 41031.*

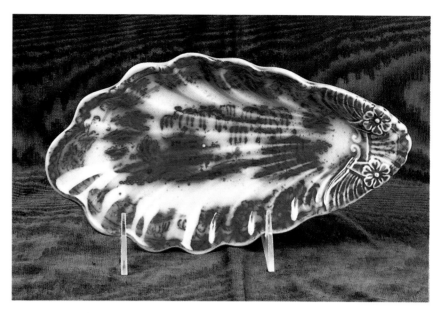

MANILLA relish dish by Podmore, Walker & Company, circa 1845. 9" long. *Courtesy of Dorothy & Elmer Caskey, Trojan Antiques, Cynthiana, Kentucky 41031.*

Large MANILLA covered bowl by Podmore, Walker & Company, circa 1845. 8" high and 10 1/4" in diameter. *Courtesy of Dorothy & Elmer Caskey, Trojan Antiques, Cynthiana, Kentucky 41031.*

MANILLA covered vegetable dish by Podmore, Walker & Company, circa 1845. 6 1/2" high, 10 1/2" x 12". *Courtesy of Dorothy & Elmer Caskey, Trojan Antiques, Cynthiana, Kentucky 41031.*

MANILLA sauce tureen and underplate by Podmore, Walker & Company, circa 1845. 6" high sauce, 6 x 7 3/4" underplate. *Courtesy of Dorothy & Elmer Caskey, Trojan Antiques, Cynthiana, Kentucky 41031.*

MANILLA gravy boat by Podmore, Walker & Company, circa 1845. *Courtesy of Dorothy & Elmer Caskey, Trojan Antiques, Cynthiana, Kentucky 41031.*

MANILLA classic gothic shape teapot, sugar bowl with lion handles, and creamer by Podmore, Walker & Company, circa 1845. 9" high teapot, 7 1/2" high sugar bowl and 5" high creamer to the spout. *Courtesy of Dorothy & Elmer Caskey, Trojan Antiques, Cynthiana, Kentucky 41031.*

MANILLA primary shape teapot, sugar, and creamer by Podmore, Walker & Company, circa 1845. *Courtesy of Dorothy & Elmer Caskey, Trojan Antiques, Cynthiana, Kentucky 41031.*

MANILLA posset cups and saucer by Podmore, Walker & Company, circa 1845. 3" high and 3" diameter cups; 5 1/4" diameter saucer. *Courtesy of Dorothy & Elmer Caskey, Trojan Antiques, Cynthiana, Kentucky 41031.*

MANILLA tea cup and saucer by Podmore, Walker & Company, circa 1845. 3" high x 3 1/2" diameter cup and 5 3/4" diameter saucer. *Courtesy of Dorothy & Elmer Caskey, Trojan Antiques, Cynthiana, Kentucky 41031.*

MANILLA waste bowl by Podmore, Walker & Company, circa 1845. 4" high, 6 1/2" in diameter. *Courtesy of Dorothy & Arnold Kowalsky.*

MANILLA sugar bowl by Podmore Walker & Company, circa 1845. 7" high. *Courtesy of Louise and Charles Loehr, Louise's Old Things, Kutztown, Pennsylvania.*

MANILLA pitcher by Podmore, Walker & Company, circa 1845. 7" high. *Courtesy of Dorothy & Elmer Caskey, Trojan Antiques, Cynthiana, Kentucky 41031.*

"Marble" sugar bowl, no manufacturer's mark. 8" high. *Courtesy of Anne & Dave Middleton, Pot O' Gold Antiques.*

MARBLE vessel by Davenport. Note the unusual dragon handle. 4" high to spout. *Courtesy of Joseph Nigro & Ralph Wick, Old Things Made New Again.*

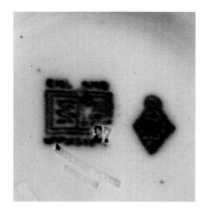

MESSINA covered butter dish, impressed Cauldon Place with a registry date of 1845. 8 3/4" dia, 5" high. *Courtesy of Dorothy & Elmer Caskey, Trojan Antiques, Cynthiana, Kentucky 41031.*

MOSS ROSE plate, no manufacturer listed, circa 1850-1860. 9 3/4" in diameter. *Courtesy of Dorothy & Elmer Caskey, Trojan Antiques, Cynthiana, Kentucky 41031.*

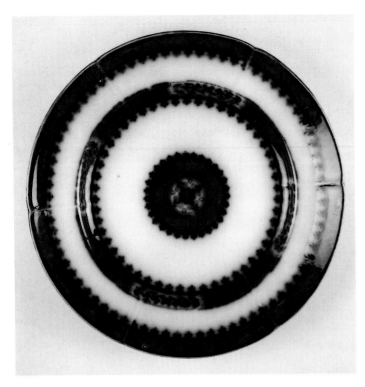

NANKIN plate by Thomas Walker. Walker produced earthenware at the Lion Works in Tunstall, Staffordshire from 1845-1851. 9 1/4" in diameter. *Courtesy of Dorothy & Arnold Kowalsky.*

NAPIER ginger jar by John & George Alcock, 1822-1859. 4" high. *Courtesy of Joseph Nigro & Ralph Wick, Old Things Made New Again.*

NAPIER potato bowl by John & George Alcock, 1822-1859. 10 1/2" in diameter *Courtesy of Joseph Nigro & Ralph Wick, Old Things Made New Again.*

NING PO platter with no back mark, circa 1845. 15 1/2" x 11 3/4". *Courtesy of Dorothy & Arnold Kowalsky.*

NING PO plate by Ralph Hall & Company. The mark dates from 1841-1849. 7 1/2" in diameter. *Courtesy of Anne & Dave Middleton, Pot O' Gold Antiques.*

OREGON pedestalled covered vegetable dish by Thomas, John & Joseph Mayer, circa 1845. 9 1/4" square, 7 1/2" high to finial. *Courtesy of Dorothy & Arnold Kowalsky.*

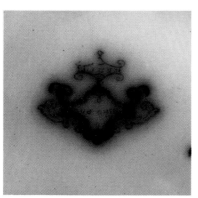

Ralph Hall & Company, Swan Bank, Tunstall, Staffordshire. The printed "R. H. & CO." manufacturers' mark dates from 1841-1849. *Courtesy of Anne & Dave Middleton, Pot O' Gold Antiques.*

OREGON waste bowl by Thomas, John & Joseph Mayer, circa 1845. 4 1/8" high, 6 1/2" in diameter. *Courtesy of Dorothy & Arnold Kowalsky.*

NING PO teapot by Ralph Hall & Company, Tunstall, Staffordshire, 1841-1849. 8 1/2" high. *Courtesy of Lucille and Norman Bagdon.*

ORIENTAL celery or condiment tray by Samuel Alcock & Company, circa 1840. 9 1/2" x 11". *Courtesy of Dorothy & Elmer Caskey, Trojan Antiques, Cynthiana, Kentucky 41031.*

ORIENTAL covered vegetable dish by Samuel Alcock & Company, circa 1840. 10 1/2" in diameter. *Courtesy of Dorothy & Elmer Caskey, Trojan Antiques, Cynthiana, Kentucky 41031.*

ORIENTAL sauce tureen with underplate by Samuel Alcock & Company, circa 1840. The tureen measures 6" high and the underplate measures 8" in diameter. *Courtesy of Dorothy & Elmer Caskey, Trojan Antiques, Cynthiana, Kentucky 41031.*

ORIENTAL, four different shapes of tea cup and handle by Samuel Alcock & Company. The cups range from 4" in diameter to 3 1/2" in diameter. *Courtesy of Dorothy & Elmer Caskey, Trojan Antiques, Cynthiana, Kentucky 41031.*

ORIENTAL teapot and creamer by Samuel Alcock & Company, circa 1844. The teapot is in a rococo style. 7" high teapot and 6" high creamer. *Courtesy of Dorothy & Elmer Caskey, Trojan Antiques, Cynthiana, Kentucky 41031.*

ORIENTAL sugar bowl and creamer by Samuel Alcock & Company, an earlier design. 6" sugar, 4 1/2" high creamer. *Courtesy of Dorothy & Elmer Caskey, Trojan Antiques, Cynthiana, Kentucky 41031.*

ORIENTAL waste bowl by Samuel Alcock & Company, circa 1840. 7 1/4" in diameter and 3 1/4" high. *Courtesy of Dorothy & Elmer Caskey, Trojan Antiques, Cynthiana, Kentucky 41031.*

ORIENTAL fruit bowl by Samuel Alcock & Company, circa 1840. 10 1/2" in diameter and 6" high. *Courtesy of Dorothy & Elmer Caskey, Trojan Antiques, Cynthiana, Kentucky 41031.*

ORIENTAL polychrome platter by Samuel Alcock & Company, circa 1840. 10 1/2" x 12 1/2". *Courtesy of Dorothy & Elmer Caskey, Trojan Antiques, Cynthiana, Kentucky 41031.*

ORIENTAL teacup and saucer in polychrome by Samuel Alcock and Company, circa 1840. The cup measures 4" in diameter and the saucer measures 6" in diameter. *Courtesy of Dorothy & Elmer Caskey, Trojan Antiques, Cynthiana, Kentucky 41031.*

PEKING teapots by William Ridgway with an 1845 date of registry. 9 1/2" high and 8 3/4" high. *Courtesy of Lucille and Norman Bagdon.*

PEKING handled tray, no manufacturers' mark and an 1845 registration mark. 8" in diameter. *Courtesy of Anne & Dave Middleton, Pot O' Gold Antiques.*

PEKING open vegetable dish, no manufacturers' mark, circa 1845. 10 1/4" x 7 3/4" x 2". *Courtesy of Anne & Dave Middleton, Pot O' Gold Antiques.*

PEKING soup tureen without a lid on the left; PEKING compote on the right. No manufacturers' mark, circa 1845. The tureen measures 11" handle to handle, 8" in diameter, and 7 1/2" high; the compote measures 8 1/2" in diameter and 6 1/4" high. *Courtesy of Joseph Nigro & Ralph Wick, Old Things Made New Again.*

"Pinwheel" plate by Charles Meigh & Sons, circa 1851. 9 1/4" in diameter. *Courtesy of Louise and Charles Loehr, Louise's Old Things, Kutztown, Pennsylvania.*

OPAQUE PORCELAIN impressed mark used from 1851-1861 alone or with other marks by Charles Meigh & Sons, Hanley, Staffordshire, England. *Courtesy of Louise and Charles Loehr, Louise's Old Things, Kutztown, Pennsylvania.*

"Prince Of Prussia, Princess Royal" commemorative pitcher. No manufacturers' mark. 4 1/4" high. *Courtesy of Joseph Nigro & Ralph Wick,
Old Things Made New Again.*

Several potters with the name Hackwood produced earthenwares and creamwares at Shelton and Hanley from 1827 to 1855 and used the "H" mark. *Courtesy of Lucille and Norman Bagdon.*

RHINE plate by Thomas Dimmock & Company, dated May 7, 1844 by the registration mark. 10 1/2" in diameter. *Courtesy of Louise and Charles Loehr, Louise's Old Things, Kutztown, Pennsylvania.*

RHONE Platter by Thomas Furnival & Company, circa 1845. 16" x 12 1/2". *Courtesy of Louise and Charles Loehr, Louise's Old Things, Kutztown, Pennsylvania.*

RHODA GARDENS platter by one of several Hackwoods, 1827-1855. 16" in diameter. *Courtesy of Lucille and Norman Bagdon.*

RHONE potato bowl by Thomas Furnival & Company, circa 1845. Variability in design is a Furnival trademark, as may be seen here. 11 7/8" in diameter. *Courtesy of Dorothy & Arnold Kowalsky.*

ROSE AND JASMINE reticulated chestnut bowl by Wedgwood with a manufacturers' mark dating to 1850. The bowl measures 12" x 8" x 3 1/2" high. The underplate measures 11" x 8 1/2". *Courtesy of Joseph Nigro & Ralph Wick, Old Things Made New Again.*

SCINDE teapot by Dimmock & Smith, circa 1842. 8" H. *Courtesy of Louise and Charles Loehr, Louise's Old Things, Kutztown, Pennsylvania.*

Dimmock & Smith, Hanley, Staffordshire, England, D & S printed manufacturers' mark used from 1842-1859 and SCINDE pattern name. *Courtesy of Louise and Charles Loehr, Louise's Old Things, Kutztown, Pennsylvania.*

SCINDE cups and saucer by John & George Alcock, circa 1840. 6"
diameter saucer. Center cup 2 3/4" high x 3 3/4" diameter; left cup 2
3/4" high x 3 1/4" diameter; right cup 3" high x 3 3/4" diameter *Courtesy of Anne & Dave Middleton, Pot O' Gold Antiques.*

SCINDE open vegetable dish by Thomas Walker, circa 1847. 7 1/4" x 5
1/8". *Courtesy of Dorothy & Arnold Kowalsky.*

Thomas Walker, Lion Works, Tunstall, Staffordshire,
printed "T. WALKER" manufacturers' mark with
"SCINDE" pattern name and "IRONSTONE" body ware
type. Walker was potting in Tunstall from 1845-1851
and this mark was used throughout the period. *Courtesy
of Anne & Dave Middleton, Pot O' Gold Antiques.*

SCINDE coffee pot by Podmore, Walker & Company, circa 1845. 9 1/2" high. *Courtesy of Lucille and Norman Bagdon.*

THE TEMPLE plate by Podmore Walker & Company, circa 1850. 9 3/4" in diameter. *Courtesy of Anne & Dave Middleton, Pot O' Gold Antiques.*

SOBRAON whey bowl, unidentified maker, circa 1850. 18" diameter *Courtesy of Joseph Nigro & Ralph Wick, Old Things Made New Again.*

TEMPLE eight-sided classic gothic shape teapot by Podmore Walker & Company, circa 1845. 9 1/8" high to the finial. *Courtesy of Dorothy & Arnold Kowalsky.*

Joseph Heath manufactured earthenwares at High Street in Tunstall from 1845-1853. Printed "J-H" manufacturers' mark in use from 1845 to 1853. *Courtesy of Dorothy & Elmer Caskey, Trojan Antiques, Cynthiana, Kentucky 41031.*

TONQUIN butter dish by Joseph Heath, 1845-1853. 7" diameter *Courtesy of Dorothy & Elmer Caskey, Trojan Antiques, Cynthiana, Kentucky 41031.*

TONQUIN ewer & basin by William Adams & Sons, circa 1845. The basin measured 12 3/4" in diameter and 4 3/4" high; the ewer measured 11 1/2" high to the spout. *Courtesy of Joseph Nigro & Ralph Wick, Old Things Made New Again.*

"Tree Of Life" syrup pitcher with a pewter lid, manufacturer unknown. 9 1/4" high to the spout. *Courtesy of Lucille and Norman Bagdon.*

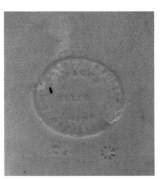

Elsmore & Forester, Tunstall, Staffordshire, England, impressed manufacturers' mark reading "ELSMORE & FORSTER, OPAQUE CHINA, TUNSTALL" around the border and the "TULIP" pattern name in the center in use from 1853-1871. The date of registry impressed on one of the pieces was 1855. *Courtesy of Louise and Charles Loehr, Louise's Old Things, Kutztown, Pennsylvania.*

TULIP creamer, teapot and sugar bowl by Elsmore & Forster, circa 1855. The teapot measured 8 3/4" high (similar in design to Elsmore & Forsters' Lustre Band pattern, *see* Snyder, *Flow Blue,* p. 70.). *Courtesy of Louise and Charles Loehr, Louise's Old Things, Kutztown, Pennsylvania.*

TULIP gravy boat and covered vegetable dish by Elsmore & Forster, circa 1860. Gravy boat measured 8 1/2" in length and 5" high; the covered vegetable dish measured 7" x 10" x 7" high. *Courtesy of Louise and Charles Loehr, Louise's Old Things, Kutztown, Pennsylvania.*

TULIP Covered Vegetable Dish Lid showing the detail of the tulip pattern. *Courtesy of Louise and Charles Loehr, Louise's Old Things, Kutztown, Pennsylvania.*

TULIP and FERN platter, unmarked with either manufacturers' mark or pattern name, circa 1850. 17 1/2" x 14". *Courtesy of Louise and Charles Loehr, Louise's Old Things, Kutztown, Pennsylvania.*

TULIP & SPRIG teapot, creamer, sugar, cup and sauser, and waste bowl by Thomas Walker, 1845. The teapot measured 9" high, the creamer 6 1/4" to spout, the sugar bowl 8 1/4" high, the handleless cup 4" in diameter, the saucer 6" in diameter, and the waste bowl 5 3/8" in diameter and 3 3/4" high. *Courtesy of Joseph Nigro & Ralph Wick, Old Things Made New Again.*

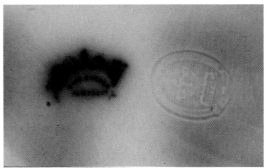

VINE BORDER by J. & M.P. Bell & Company (Ltd.), circa 1850. 11 x 8 1/2". *Courtesy of Dorothy & Arnold Kowalsky.*

J. & M.P. Bell & Co. (Ltd.), Glassgow Pottery, Dobbies Loan, Glasgow, Sxcotland, 1842-1928. The printed "J&MPB&CO." initials were used from circa 1850-70. *Courtesy of Dorothy & Arnold Kowalsky.*

VINE BORDER platter by Davenport, circa 1850. 14 3/4" x 11 3/4".
*Courtesy of Joseph Nigro & Ralph Wick, Old Things Made New Again.*

Mellor, Venables & Company, Hole House Pottery, Burslem,
Staffordshire. The company produced earthenwares and china
from 1834-1851. Impressed manufacturers' mark and printed
"WHAMPOA" pattern name. *Courtesy of Dorothy & Arnold
Kowalsky.*

WHAMPOA paneled plate by Mellor, Venables & Company, circa 1845.
The plate measures 10 1/4" in diameter. *Courtesy of Anne & Dave
Middleton, Pot O' Gold Antiques.*

WHAMPOA platter by Mellor, Venables & Company, circa
1845. 13" x 9 1/2". *Courtesy of Dorothy & Arnold Kowalsky.*

WHAMPOA well and tree platter by Mellor, Venables & Company, circa 1845. 20 3/4". *Courtesy of Lucille and Norman Bagdon.*

WHAMPOA covered vegetable dish by Mellor, Venables & Company with gold trim, circa 1845. *Courtesy of Lucille and Norman Bagdon.*

WAMPHOA tyg by Mellor, Venables & Company with gold trim, circa 1845. 4 7/8" diameter. *Courtesy of Joseph Nigro & Ralph Wick, Old Things Made New Again.*

WHAMPOA tygs by Mellor, Venables & Company, circa 1845. The large tyg measured 4 3/4" in diameter and 4 3/4" high. The smaller tyg measured 3 1/4" in diameter and 3 1/8" high. *Courtesy of Joseph Nigro & Ralph Wick, Old Things Made New Again.*

## The Middle Victorian Period: 1860 to 1880

During the Middle Victorian period, the fascination for the natural world escalated, Japanese decorative motifs became popular in the West, and the Aesthetic Movement began — decrying the blight of the technological age. All these events influenced the appearance of Flow Blue.

In other affairs, by 1861 the population of Great Britain reached the 23 million mark while the United States population topped 32 million. Between 1861 and 1865 the United States of America attempted to tear itself in two while disentangling itself from the horrors of slavery and settling a long standing states rights debate through the bloody battles of the Civil War. In 1865 America ended its destructive conflict, remaining united but losing Abraham Lincoln, the first American president to be assassinated.[3]

In other fields of endeavor, 1865 saw the first train holdup in North Bend, Ohio and the invention of the ice machine by Thaddeus Love. Meanwhile, 1865 also found adults reading Lewis Carroll's "Alice's Adventures in Wonderland" to their children for the first time. By the end of the Middle Victorian period, Britain has fought the Zulu War of 1879. In 1880 France annexed Tahiti, T.A. Edison and J.W. Swan both independently devise the first practical electric lights, the United States boasted 87,800 miles of railroad lines, James A. Garfield was elected the 20th President of the United States, and families sat down to their first canned meats and fruits ever. Some may have been served on Flow Blue.[4]

BLUE BELL syrup pitcher with pewter lid by James Dixon, circa 1860. 10 1/4" high. *Courtesy of Dorothy & Elmer Caskey, Trojan Antiques, Cynthiana, Kentucky 41031.*

BLUE BELL mugs, no manufacturers' mark, circa 1860, each with different handles. 4 1/2", 3 1/2", and 3 1/4" high. *Courtesy of Dorothy & Elmer Caskey, Trojan Antiques, Cynthiana, Kentucky 41031.*

BLUE BELL jam dish with lion finial and handles, no manufacturers' mark, circa 1860. 5" in diameter and 4 1/2" high. *Courtesy of Joseph Nigro & Ralph Wick, Old Things Made New Again.*

BLUE BELL candlesticks, no manufacturers' mark, circa 1860. 7 1/4" & 9 1/4" high. *Courtesy of Dorothy & Elmer Caskey, Trojan Antiques, Cynthiana, Kentucky 41031.*

BLUE BELL hot creamer, no manufacturers' mark, circa 1860. 4 3/4" high to the spout. *Courtesy of Joseph Nigro & Ralph Wick, Old Things Made New Again.*

BLUE BELL pitchers, no manufacturers' mark, circa 1860. Note the unusual lip designs. 6" and 7 3/4" high. *Courtesy of Dorothy & Elmer Caskey, Trojan Antiques, Cynthiana, Kentucky 41031.*

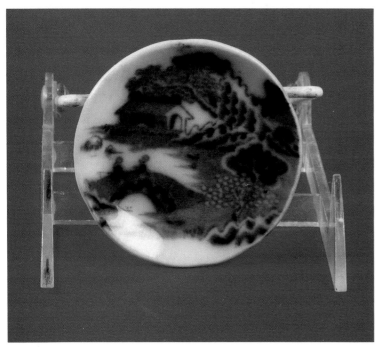

CHINESE LANDSCAPE butter pat by George L.& Taylor Ashworth. Impressed "ASHWORTH REAL IRONSTONE CHINA" in use from 1862 to 1880. 3" in diameter. *Courtesy of Dorothy & Elmer Caskey, Trojan Antiques, Cynthiana, Kentucky 41031.*

CHINESE LANDSCAPE soup tureen by George L.& Taylor Ashworth, circa 1862. Marked "Mason's Patent Ironstone China." 9 1/2" high. *Courtesy of Dorothy & Elmer Caskey, Trojan Antiques, Cynthiana, Kentucky 41031.*

CHINESE LANDSCAPE fruit bowl by George L.& Taylor Ashworth, circa 1862. Marked "Mason's Real Ironstone China." 5 3/4" high. *Courtesy of Dorothy & Elmer Caskey, Trojan Antiques, Cynthiana, Kentucky 41031.*

CHINESE LANDSCAPE sauce tureen and underplate by George L.& Taylor Ashworth, circa 1862. Marked "Mason's Real Ironstone China." 6" high. *Courtesy of Dorothy & Elmer Caskey, Trojan Antiques, Cynthiana, Kentucky 41031.*

DAMASK ROSE well & tree platter by Davenport, 1860. 21" x 16 1/2". *Courtesy of Joseph Nigro & Ralph Wick, Old Things Made New Again.*

FORMOSA fruit bowl by Frederick Jones (& Co.), Stafford Street (circa 1865-1873), and Chadwick Street (circa 1868-1886), Longton. The mark "F. JONES LONGTON" is found on several impressed and printed marks on earthenwares from 1865-1886. 10 1/4" in diameter. *Courtesy of Dorothy & Elmer Caskey, Trojan Antiques, Cynthiana, Kentucky 41031.*

FORMOSA pedestalled compote by Frederick Jones, 1870. 13 1/4" x 10 1/4" x 7 3/8" high. *Courtesy of Joseph Nigro & Ralph Wick, Old Things Made New Again.*

GEM plate by Ralph Hammersley (& Son), circa 1868. This plate would have been very popular in a United States trying to heal the wounds of the Civil War. Patriotic symbols always are more popular in troubled times. 8 3/4" diameter. *Courtesy of Joseph Nigro & Ralph Wick, Old Things Made New Again.*

INDIAN EMPRESS small oval undertray with gold trim, Brown Westhead, Moore & Company with mark and impress. This piece has an 1877 registration date. 8 3/8" x 6 3/8". *Courtesy of Dorothy & Arnold Kowalsky.*

Ralph Hammersley (& Son), Overhouse Pottery (circa 1880+), Burslem; Church Bank Pottery, Tunstall, circa 1860-1883; and Black Works, Tunstall, circa 1885-1888. The pottery was producing earthenwares from 1860-1905. This mark has an 1868 registration mark. *Courtesy of Joseph Nigro & Ralph Wick, Old Things Made New Again.*

JAPAN cup and saucer, Thomas Fell & Co., circa 1860. The cup measures 4" in diameter and 2 1/4" high; the saucer measures 5 5/8" in diameter. *Courtesy of Joseph Nigro & Ralph Wick, Old Things Made New Again.*

MONGOLIA open vegetable dish with "F & W" printed back mark, circa 1850s-1860s. 10" square. *Courtesy of Joseph Nigro & Ralph Wick, Old Things Made New Again.*

MONGOLIA wash basin and pitcher, marked "F & W", circa 1850s-1860s. The basin measures 12 3/4" in diameter; the pitcher measures 10" high to the spout. *Courtesy of Joseph Nigro & Ralph Wick, Old Things Made New Again.*

The "F & W" printed mark is found with pattern names on printed marks on mid-nineteenth century earthenwares. According to Geoffrey Godden, the initials do not fit any of the Staffordshire potters. They may relate to a foreign retailer.[8] *Courtesy of Joseph Nigro & Ralph Wick, Old Things Made New Again.*

MORNING GLORY family size egg cup holder set, no manufacturers' mark, circa 1870. *Courtesy of Dorothy & Elmer Caskey, Trojan Antiques, Cynthiana, Kentucky 41031.*

"Nautilus Shell" vase, Pinder, Bourne & Company, 1862. 5 1/2" high, 7 1/2" long. *Courtesy of Joseph Nigro & Ralph Wick, Old Things Made New Again.*

SHELL milk pitcher by Edward Challinor (1842-1867), circa 1860. 6 1/2" high to the spout. *Courtesy of Lucille and Norman Bagdon.*

**PINDER BOURNE & C°**

Pinder, Bourne & Company manufacturers' mark, Nile Street, Burslem, produced earthenwares from January 1862 to 1882. *Courtesy of Joseph Nigro & Ralph Wick, Old Things Made New Again.*

PERSIANNA platter by G. L. Ashworth, circa 1862. 21 1/2". *Courtesy of Lucille and Norman Bagdon.*

SHELL sugar bowl bearing no manufacturers' mark, circa 1860. 7 1/2" high. *Courtesy of Dorothy & Elmer Caskey, Trojan Antiques, Cynthiana, Kentucky 41031.*

Shell Gravy Boat bearing neither manufacturers' mark nor pattern name, circa 1860. 4 1/2" x 7 1/2". *Courtesy of Louise and Charles Loehr, Louise's Old Things, Kutztown, Pennsylvania.*

SIMLA soup tureen by Elsmore & Forster, circa 1860. 12" x 9" x 11" high. *Courtesy of Joseph Nigro & Ralph Wick, Old Things Made New Again.*

Unidentified pattern on a whey bowl by John Carr & Sons, Northshields, dating to circa 1861. 14 5/8" x 1 7/8". *Courtesy of Dorothy & Arnold Kowalsky.*

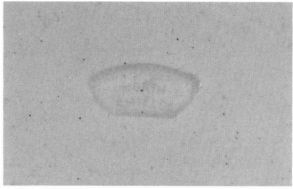

John Carr (& Co.)(& Sons) of Low Lights Pottery in North Shields, Northumberland produced earthenwares from circa 1845-1900. The style of the mark was changed to "& Sons" in 1861. *Courtesy of Dorothy & Arnold Kowalsky.*

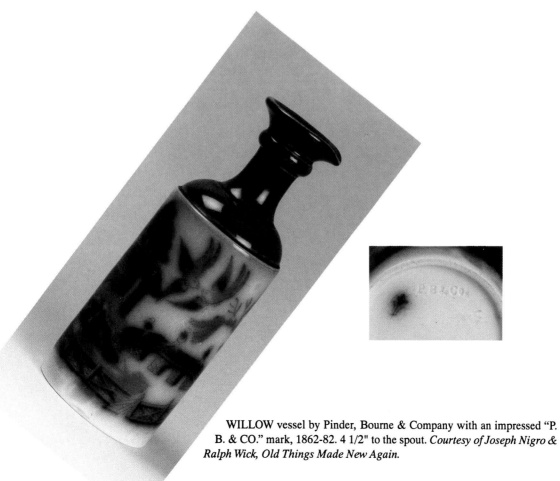

WILLOW vessel by Pinder, Bourne & Company with an impressed "P. B. & CO." mark, 1862-82. 4 1/2" to the spout. *Courtesy of Joseph Nigro & Ralph Wick, Old Things Made New Again.*

## The Late Victorian Period: 1880 to the Early Twentieth Century

By the Late Victorian, fancy embellishments and excessive decoration wane early under the influence of the Arts and Crafts movement. Later Art Nouveau provides a final touch of stylized natural forms to Flow Blue design which W.B. Honey would proclaim was so much "school-taught curliness."

Additionally, the newly elected President James A. Garfield died in 1881 from the ministrations of physicians attempting to save him from a would-be assassins bullet. Also in 1881 the Canadian Pacific Railway Company was formed, Tchaikovsky's "1812 Overture" was performed, and swash-buckling adventure filled Victorian minds as they read Robert Louis Stevenson's newly printed "Treasure Island." In 1883 American frontiersman W.F. Cody, a.k.a. "Buffalo Bill," organized his "Wild West Show." A decade later, in 1893, Henry Ford built his first car. England celebrated Queen Victoria's Diamond Jubilee in 1897. Passing from the nineteenth century to the twentieth, William McKinley, the United States 25th President, is reelected and the Zepplin made its first trial flight.[5]

The "century of steam" passed for the "century of electricity" in 1901, taking with it both Queen Victoria and William McKinley. The Queen was succeeded by her son Edward VII while the President was succeeded by Theodore Roosevelt. In 1902 literate adults were thrilled and mystified by A. Conan Doyle's newly released Sherlock Holmes mystery "The Hound of the Baskervilles" while their children devoured Beatrix Potters' "Peter Rabbit." Finally, in 1903 the Alaskan frontier was settled, the first American trans-continental road trip was made by car — taking 65 days, Britain established a 20 mile-per-hour speed limit for English motor cars, and Orville and Wilbur Wright successfully flew a powered airplane. While Flow Blue would continue to be produced for a while longer, this is a fine place to stop.[6]

ADELAIDE by Doulton, circa 1898 with 1895 and 1898 registration dates. 6" diameter with two registration numbers. *Courtesy of Dorothy & Arnold Kowalsky.*

ADDERLEY open vegetable by Doulton with luster trim and gold, circa 1886. 8 1/2" x 8 3/4", 2 3/4". *Courtesy of Dorothy & Arnold Kowalsky.*

AMHERST JAPAN farmers (breakfast mush) cup and saucer with polychrome overglaze by Minton. A year cypher on the saucer dates this piece to 1920. The saucer measures 9" in diameter. The cup measures 4" high and 5 3/8" in diameter. *Courtesy of Dorothy & Arnold Kowalsky.*

ATLAS tea tiles by W.H. Grindley & Company, circa 1880-1914. 6 5/8" x 6 3/8" diameter with backmark. *Courtesy of Dorothy & Arnold Kowalsky.*

ARGYLE spooner by W.H. Grindley & Company. The back mark dates this piece from circa 1880-1914. 5 1/4" high x 3 1/2" in diameter. *Courtesy of Dorothy & Arnold Kowalsky.*

Ford & Sons (Ltd.), Newcastle Street, Burslem, Staffordshire, produced under this name from circa 1893-1938. After 1938 the firm became Ford & Sons (Crownford) Ltd. This printed mark dates from circa 1893 on. Ltd. was added to at times from 1908 onward. *Courtesy of Anne & Dave Middleton, Pot O' Gold Antiques.*

AVON teapot and stand by Ford & Sons (Ltd.), circa 1893 onward. Stand measures 6 1/2" x 6"; the teapot measures 7" high. *Courtesy of Anne & Dave Middleton, Pot O' Gold Antiques.*

BRAZIL platter by W.H. Grindley & Company, circa 1891. 14 1/4" x 10 1/2". *Courtesy of Dorothy & Arnold Kowalsky.*

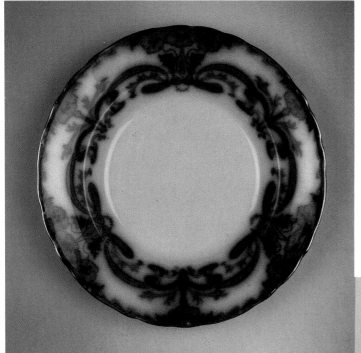

BURLEIGH bowl by Burgess & Leigh, circa 1903. 10 1/2" in diameter. *Courtesy of Louise and Charles Loehr, Louise's Old Things, Kutztown, Pennsylvania.*

CECIL demitasse cup and saucer by Till & Sons, circa 1891. The cup measures 2 3/4" in diameter and 2" high; the saucer measures 5" in diameter. *Courtesy of Joseph Nigro & Ralph Wick, Old Things Made New Again.*

Till & Sons, Sytch Pottery, Burslem, Staffordshire produced earthenwares from circa 1850-1928. This manufacturers mark dates from circa 1880, however the addition of ENGLAND dates the mark from 1891 onward. *Courtesy of Joseph Nigro & Ralph Wick, Old Things Made New Again.*

CHELSEA pitchers by Bishop and Stonier, circa 1900. 7 1/4", 7 3/4", 8 1/4" high to the spout. *Courtesy of Lucille and Norman Bagdon.*

CHUSAN cheese dish by Wiltshaw & Robinson (Ltd.), circa 1899. *Courtesy of Dorothy & Elmer Caskey, Trojan Antiques, Cynthiana, Kentucky 41031.*

Wiltshaw & Robinson (Ltd.), Carlton Works, Stoke, Staffordshire, produced earthenwares and china from 1890 to 1957. This particular mark dates from circa 1894 onwards and the date of registry indicated by the registration number below the mark was 1899. *Courtesy of Dorothy & Elmer Caskey, Trojan Antiques, Cynthiana, Kentucky 41031.*

CHUSAN drainer by Wedgwood, rare, circa 1882. This pattern was produced by Wedgwood in three periods of the 1840s-50s, the 1860s and the 1880s. This example was exported to Scotland. 10 7/8" in diameter. *Courtesy of Dorothy & Arnold Kowalsky.*

CHUSAN nested plates by Wedgwood, circa 1882. 10 1/2", 9 1/2", and 8 3/4" in diameter. *Courtesy of Dorothy & Arnold Kowalsky.*

CHUSAN sauce tureen with a tab handled attached undertray by Wedgwood, circa 1882. The undertray measures 8 1/2" x 7 1/2" and the entire tureen measures 7" high. *Courtesy of Dorothy & Arnold Kowalsky.*

CHUSAN covered vegetable by Wedgwood, circa 1882. 11" x 10 1/4" x 6 1/2" high. *Courtesy of Dorothy & Arnold Kowalsky.*

CHUSAN gravy boat with an attached undertray by Wedgwood, circa 1882. 7" x 5" base. *Courtesy of Dorothy & Arnold Kowalsky.*

CLAREMONT covered vegetable dish by Johnson Brothers, circa 1891. 11" x 9" in diameter, 6 1/2" high. *Courtesy of Dorothy & Arnold Kowalsky*

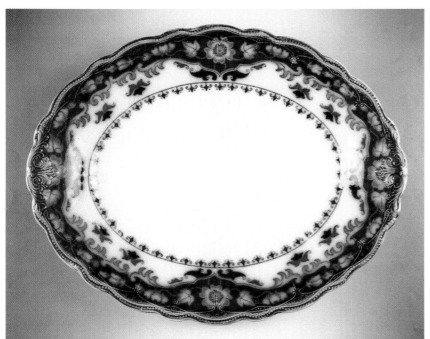

CRUMLIN platter by Myott, Son & Co. (Ltd.), circa 1900+. *Courtesy of Dorothy & Arnold Kowalsky.*

Myott, Son & Co. (Ltd.), Alexander Pottery, Stoke (1898-1902), Cobridge (1902-1946), and Hanley (circa 1947- ). This mark was in use by Myott, Son & Co. (Ltd.) from circa 1900+. *Courtesy of Dorothy & Arnold Kowalsky.*

CRUMLIN sauce tureen by Myott, Son & Co. (Ltd.), circa 1900+. The underplate measures 8 3/4" x 6 3/4". The tureen measures 5" high. *Courtesy of Lucille and Norman Bagdon.*

DEVA compartmented bon bon dish by Bourne & Leigh (Ltd.) with a manufacturers' mark dating to circa 1912+. 11 7/8". *Courtesy of Dorothy & Arnold Kowalsky.*

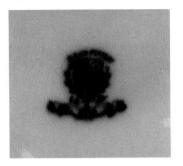

Bourne & Leigh (Ltd.), Albion Pottery, Burslem, Staffordshire produced earthenwares from 1892-1914. *Courtesy of Dorothy & Arnold Kowalsky.*

DUDLEY milk pitcher by Ford & Sons, circa 1893 onward. 8 1/2" high. *Courtesy of Anne & Dave Middleton, Pot O' Gold Antiques.*

DUDLEY covered vegetable dish, Ford & Sons, circa 1893 onward. Handle to handle the dish measures 12 1/2" x 8". *Courtesy of Dorothy & Arnold Kowalsky.*

EGLINTON TOURNAMENT commemorative pitcher by Doulton, with a registry date of 1907. 5" high to the spout. *Courtesy of Lucille and Norman Bagdon.*

FAIRY VILLAS teapot by William Adams & Company, circa 1891. 6" high. *Courtesy of Lucille and Norman Bagdon.*

FLORIS cheese dish with lid by Ford & Sons, 1891. 9 3/4" x 8 1/4" x 6 1/2" high. *Courtesy of Joseph Nigro & Ralph Wick, Old Things Made New Again.*

FRUIT BASKET drainer,
maker unknown, circa 1880.
13 1/2" x 10". *Courtesy of
Lucille and Norman Bagdon.*

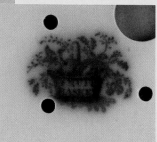

GALLEON pitcher by Doulton, circa 1891. 6" high. *Courtesy of Lucille
and Norman Bagdon.*

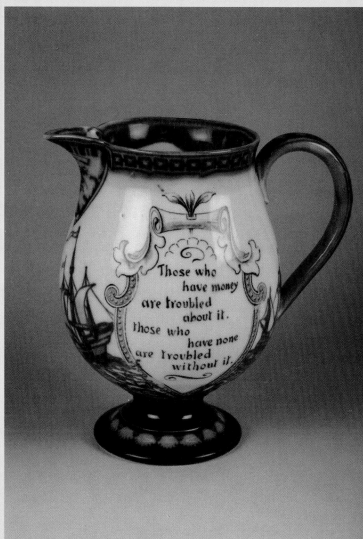

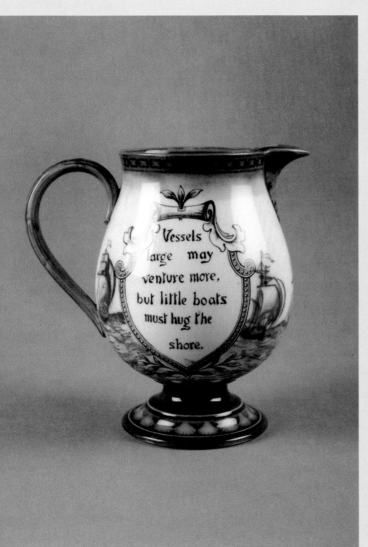

GALLEON pitcher by Doulton, circa 1891. 6 7/8" high. *Courtesy of Dorothy & Arnold Kowalsky.*

GARLAND dresser set covered powder box by William Adams & Company, circa 1891. 2 1/2" high and 2 5/8" in diameter. *Courtesy of Dorothy & Arnold Kowalsky.*

GLOIRE-DE DIJON toothbrush holder by Doulton, circa 1891. Tooth-brush holders range from 4" to 7" high. *Courtesy of Dorothy & Arnold Kowalsky.*

GLORIE DE DEJON pitcher by Doulton. This piece has a registry date of 1897, Rd. No. 307615. 7" high. *Courtesy of Dorothy & Arnold Kowalsky.*

GOUCHOS covered vegetable, unidentified manufacturer, the mark is dated from 1890 onward by the presence of the term "WARRENTED" in the mark. 12 3/4" x 9 1/4". *Courtesy of Joseph Nigro & Ralph Wick, Old Things Made New Again.*

KEELE oval covered vegetable dish by W.H. Grindley, circa 1891. 12 1/8" x 7 3/4" handle to handle and 6" high. *Courtesy of Dorothy & Arnold Kowalsky.*

HAMILTON sauce ladle by John Maddock & Son. The sauce ladle post-dates 1909 with registration number 566775. *Courtesy of Dorothy & Arnold Kowalsky.*

IRIS three chambered dish by Doulton, circa 1891. The dish measures roughly 11" across. *Courtesy of Dorothy & Elmer Caskey, Trojan Antiques, Cynthiana, Kentucky 41031.*

KENDAL tray by Ridgways, circa 1912. 8 1/4" x 5 1/4". *Courtesy of Louise and Charles Loehr, Louise's Old Things, Kutztown, Pennsylvania.*

KYBER small "sauce tureen" with undertray by William Adams & Company, circa 1891. 8" high. *Courtesy of Louise and Charles Loehr, Louise's Old Things, Kutztown, Pennsylvania.*

KYBER wash basin and pitcher by William Adams & Company, circa 1891. The pitcher has eight cuts and six panels on a pedestalled base, measuring 10 1/4" to the spout. The basin has twelve cuts around the edge and measures 14" in diameter. *Courtesy of Dorothy & Arnold Kowalsky.*

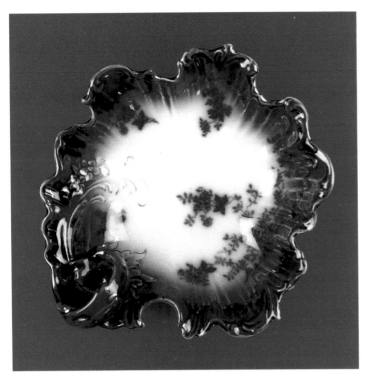

"La Belle" handled dish by the Wheeling Pottery Company, 1893. 10" x 9 1/2" x 2 1/2" high. *Courtesy of Anne & Dave Middleton, Pot O' Gold Antiques.*

LE PAVO punch cup by W.H. Grindley & Company. The registry number dates to 1896. 3" high and 3" in diameter. *Courtesy of Dorothy & Arnold Kowalsky.*

"La Belle" ice cream dish by the Wheeling Pottery Company, 1893. 13 1/2" x 4 5/8" x 2 1/4" high. *Courtesy of Dorothy & Arnold Kowalsky.*

"La Belle" bread tray by the Wheeling Pottery Company, 1893. 14 1/2" x 6 1/8". *Courtesy of Dorothy & Arnold Kowalsky.*

LINCOLN platter by Bishop & Stonier, 1891-1936, 21 x 17". *Courtesy of Dorothy & Elmer Caskey, Trojan Antiques, Cynthiana, Kentucky 41031.*

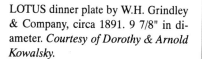

LOTUS dinner plate by W.H. Grindley & Company, circa 1891. 9 7/8" in diameter. *Courtesy of Dorothy & Arnold Kowalsky.*

LINCOLN plate by Bishop & Stonier, 1891-1936, 10 1/4" diameter Mark as well. *Courtesy of Dorothy & Elmer Caskey, Trojan Antiques, Cynthiana, Kentucky 41031.*

MADRAS well & tree by Doulton, circa 1891. 19 6/8" x 16". *Courtesy of Dorothy & Arnold Kowalsky.*

MADRAS individual vegetable dish by Doulton, circa 1891. *Courtesy of Dorothy & Arnold Kowalsky.*

MADRAS place setting with and without gold including tea and dessert service sizes by Doulton, circa 1891. 10 1/2", 9 1/2", 8 1/2", 7 1/2", 6 3/8", and 5 1/2" in diameter. *Courtesy of Dorothy & Arnold Kowalsky.*

MADRAS potato bowl by Doulton, circa 1891. 9 7/8" in diameter. *Courtesy of Dorothy & Arnold Kowalsky.*

MADRAS bone dish which went with the fish service, by Doulton, circa 1891. 6". *Courtesy of Dorothy & Arnold Kowalsky.*

MADRAS berry dishes by Doulton, circa 1891. 4 7/8", 5 1/4", and 6 1/8" in diameter. *Courtesy of Dorothy & Arnold Kowalsky.*

MADRAS three nested open vegetable dishes by Doulton, circa 1891. 10 1/2", 7 7/8" and 9 5/8" x 7 1/4". *Courtesy of Dorothy & Arnold Kowalsky.*

MADRAS coffee cup, tea cup, two handled bullion cup, punch cup, and demitasse cup by Doulton, circa 1891. *Courtesy of Dorothy & Arnold Kowalsky.*

MADRAS egg cups by Doulton, circa 1891. The double egg measures 3 7/8" high, the pigeon egg 2 1/2" high, and the quail egg (smallest) 2 1/4" high. *Courtesy of Dorothy & Arnold Kowalsky.*

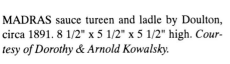

MADRAS sauce tureen and ladle by Doulton, circa 1891. 8 1/2" x 5 1/2" x 5 1/2" high. *Courtesy of Dorothy & Arnold Kowalsky.*

MADRAS round soup tureen with ladle by Doulton, circa 1891. 11 5/8" diameter undertray. 11 1/2" x 10" x 6.5" high tureen. *Courtesy of Dorothy & Arnold Kowalsky.*

MADRAS round and oval vegetable dishes and a gravy boat with undertray by Doulton, 1891. The round dish measures 9 7/8" across the handles x 8 3/4" in diameter x 6 1/2" high. The oval dish measures 11 7/8" x 7 1/2" x 6 1/2" high. The gravy boat measures 8 1/4" across x 3 1/2" high. *Courtesy of Dorothy & Arnold Kowalsky.*

MADRAS undertrays by Doulton, circa 1891. The sauce undertray measures 8 1/2" x 6 1/4"; the gravy 8" x 5"; the tab handled gravy 7 5/8" x 5 1/8". *Courtesy of Dorothy & Arnold Kowalsky.*

MADRAS covered butter with drainer by Doulton, circa 1891. *Courtesy of Dorothy & Arnold Kowalsky.*

A set of eight graduated MADRAS pitchers by Doulton, circa 1891. From the smallest to the larges the measures to the spout: 3 3/4", 4 1/2", 5 1/2", 6", 7", 7 1/2", 8 1/2", and 8 1/2" high. The largest has a double loop handle. *Courtesy of Dorothy & Arnold Kowalsky.*

MADRAS teapots and a tea tile by Doulton, circa 1891. The teapots measure to the spouts from the largest to the smallest: 4 3/4", 4 1/4" (full size, first two), 4" (third - breakfast tea for two), 3 1/2" (fourth - child's teapot). The tile measures 6" in diameter. *Courtesy of Dorothy & Arnold Kowalsky.*

MADRAS platter, possibly manufactured by Wood & Baggaley, Hill Works, Burslem, Staffordshire 1870-1880 with the "W & B" manufacturers' mark. *Courtesy of Dorothy & Arnold Kowalsky.*

MARGUERITE covered vegetable dish by W.H. Grindley & Company, circa 1891. 6" high. *Courtesy of Anne & Dave Middleton, Pot O' Gold Antiques.*

MARECHAL NEIL open vegetable dish by W.H. Grindley & Company, circa 1895. 9 3/4" x 7 1/8" x 1 1/2" high. *Courtesy of Dorothy & Arnold Kowalsky.*

MELROSE sauce ladle by Doulton, circa 1891. *Courtesy of Dorothy & Arnold Kowalsky.*

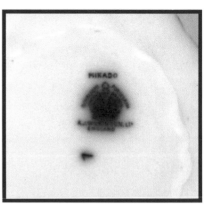

Arthur J. Wilkinson, Ltd. produced earthenwares and ironstones at the Royal Staffordshire Pottery, Burslem from 1885 onward. This mark was produced after circa 1896 when "Ltd." was added to the Wilkinson marks. *Courtesy of Dorothy & Arnold Kowalsky.*

MIKADO teapot by A.J. Wilkinson, Ltd., circa 1896. 7" high. *Courtesy of Dorothy & Arnold Kowalsky.*

NAPOLI tureen by Burgess & Leigh, circa 1912. 12 3/4" x 8 3/4" x 7 3/4" high. 2 1/2 quart. *Courtesy of Louise and Charles Loehr, Louise's Old Things, Kutztown, Pennsylvania.*

NORMANDY platter by Johnson Bros, circa 1900. 14" x 10 1/2". *Courtesy of Dorothy & Arnold Kowalsky.*

NORMANDY berry bowl by Johnson Brothers, circa 1900. 5" in diameter. *Courtesy of Louise and Charles Loehr, Louise's Old Things, Kutztown, Pennsylvania.*

PEACH teacup saucer by Johnson Brothers, circa 1900. 6 1/4" in diameter. *Courtesy of Dorothy & Arnold Kowalsky.*

ORIENTAL teapot by Ridgway with a reissued beehive and urn printed manufacturers' mark post-dating 1891. *Courtesy of Dorothy & Arnold Kowalsky.*

Empire Porcelain Company, Stoke, Staffordshire, post 1896 manufacturers' mark. The Empire Porcelain Company (Ltd.) has produced earthenwares at the Empire Works in Stoke since 1896. *Courtesy of Louise and Charles Loehr, Louise's Old Things, Kutztown, Pennsylvania.*

PEKIN creamer by Arthur J. Wilkinson, including a printed Royal Staffordshire Pottery manufacturers' mark, circa 1909. 3 1/2" to the spout. *Courtesy of Joseph Nigro & Ralph Wick, Old Things Made New Again.*

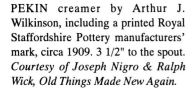

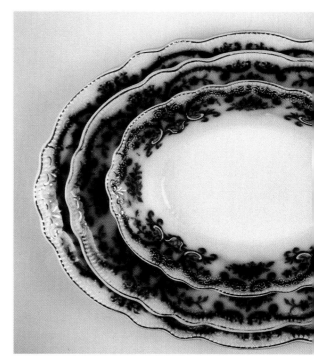

PORTMAN platters (2) and an open vegetable dish by W.H. Grindley & Company, circa 1891. The platters measures 14" x 10 1/4", 12" x 9", and the open vegetable measures 9 1/8" x 1 3/4" high. *Courtesy of Dorothy & Arnold Kowalsky.*

"Pomegranate" potpourri holder by the Empire Porcelain Company, circa 1896. 4" high and 8" in diameter. *Courtesy of Louise and Charles Loehr, Louise's Old Things, Kutztown, Pennsylvania.*

PORTMAN plates, a butter pat, a bone dish, and a gravy boat with undertray and gold trim by W.H. Grindley, circa 1891. The plates measure 9", 7 3/4", and 6 3/4" in diameter. The soup dish measures 7 3/4" in diameter, the bone dish measures 7 1/8" in diameter, the butter pat measures 3 1/8" in diameter, the undertray measures 8 3/4" x 5", and the gravy boat measures 3 1/8" to the spout. *Courtesy of Dorothy & Arnold Kowalsky.*

PORTMAN round and oval vegetable dishes by W.H. Grindley, circa 1891. The round vegetable dish measures 10 7/8" x 8 1/2"; the oval: 12 3/8" x 7 1/4"; the cup measures 3 3/4" in diameter and 2 1/4" high, and the saucer measures 5 3/4" in diameter. *Courtesy of Dorothy & Arnold Kowalsky.*

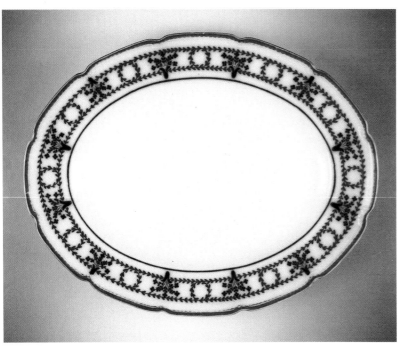

THE REGAL platter by W.H. Grindley, circa 1891. 16" x 12 1/2". *Courtesy of Dorothy & Arnold Kowalsky.*

RENOWN sauce ladle by Arthur J. Wilkinson, circa 1885. *Courtesy of Dorothy & Arnold Kowalsky.*

ROSE sauce ladle, Bourne and Leigh (Ltd.), circa 1892. Bourne and Leigh (Ltd.) produced earthenwares at the Albion and Leighton Potteries in Burslem from 1892-1941. *Courtesy of Dorothy & Arnold Kowalsky.*

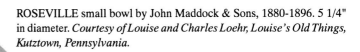

ROSEVILLE small bowl by John Maddock & Sons, 1880-1896. 5 1/4" in diameter. *Courtesy of Louise and Charles Loehr, Louise's Old Things, Kutztown, Pennsylvania.*

RUINS platter by G. L. Ashworth, circa 1880. 23" x 17 1/4". *Courtesy of Dorothy & Arnold Kowalsky.*

ROXBURY soup ladle by Ford & Sons, circa 1891. *Courtesy of Dorothy & Arnold Kowalsky.*

SIAM drainer, sets came normally with three sizes and in round, oval and rectangular shapes. The drainer sat on a platter for fish. Manufactured by T. Rathbone & Co., circa 1912+. 13" x 10". *Courtesy of Dorothy & Arnold Kowalsky.*

T. Rathbone & Company produced earthenwares at the Newfield Pottery in Tunstall from 1898-1923. This mark dates from circa 1912+. *Courtesy of Dorothy & Arnold Kowalsky.*

ROYSTON plate by Johnson Bros. Ltd., circa 1913+. 10" in diameter. *Courtesy of Louise and Charles Loehr, Louise's Old Things, Kutztown, Pennsylvania.*

SNOWFLOWER flower vase, no manufacturers mark or pattern name, circa 1891. 5 1/2" high. *Courtesy of Anne & Dave Middleton, Pot O' Gold Antiques.*

**SNOWFLOWER** decorative knick-knack impressed "Made in England",
circa 1891. 8 1/4" high. *Courtesy of Dorothy & Arnold Kowalsky.*

"Spinach" hand painted plate by Libertas, unmarked, dating from circa 1900. 7 1/4" in diameter. *Courtesy of Louise and Charles Loehr, Louise's Old Things, Kutztown, Pennsylvania.*

"STRATFORD" dresser tray with gold, Middleport Pottery with registry number 406612 dating from 1903. 12 1/4" x 9 1/2". *Courtesy of Dorothy & Arnold Kowalsky.*

TALLI platter with an unidentified "J & R CO." printed mark. 15 1/2" x 12 1/8". *Courtesy of Dorothy & Arnold Kowalsky.*

TEDWORTH sauce tureen with ladle, William Adams & Company, circa 1892. 5 5/8" x 7 7/8" x 5" high. *Courtesy of Louise and Charles Loehr, Louise's Old Things, Kutztown, Pennsylvania.*

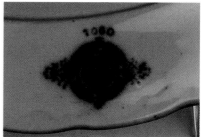

F. Winkle & Company (Ltd.), Stoke, Staffordshire, printed manufacturers' mark reading "COLONIAL POTTERY STOKE ENGLAND" around the central circle with the monogram "F. W. & CO." in the center, in use from 1890-1925. The "TOGO" pattern name is located above the mark. *Courtesy of Louise and Charles Loehr, Louise's Old Things, Kutztown, Pennsylvania.*

TOGO platter by F. Winkle & Company, circa 1900. 10" x 7 1/2". *Courtesy of Louise and Charles Loehr, Louise's Old Things, Kutztown, Pennsylvania.*

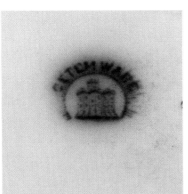

Unidentified pattern bowl by C.T. Maling & Sons (Ltd.), circa 1908+. A & B Ford Potteries, Newcastle upon Tyne, Northumberland, 1890 - 1963. This mark circa 1908+. "CETEMWARE" 8 panels, 9" dia x 3 3/4" high. *Courtesy of Dorothy & Arnold Kowalsky.*

C.T. Maling & Sons (Ltd.), A & B Ford Potteries, Newcastle upon Tyne, Northumberland, 1890-1963. This printed manufacturers' mark dates from circa 1908+. "CETEMWARE" refers to the body pattern rather than the printed pattern. 8 panels, 9" in diameter and 3 3/4" high. *Courtesy of Dorothy & Arnold Kowalsky.*

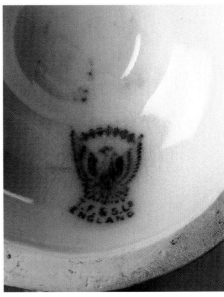

Thomas Forester & Sons (Ltd.), Phoenix Works, Longton, Staffordshire, 1883-1959, printed manufacturers' mark dating from 1891-1912 featuring the Phoenix bird and the printed "T. F. & S. Ld." initials. *Courtesy of Dorothy & Arnold Kowalsky.*

Unidentified pattern jardiniere by Thomas Forester & Sons Ltd., 1891-1912. 15" high. *Courtesy of Dorothy & Arnold Kowalsky.*

Unidentified pattern urn by Thomas Forester & Sons Ltd., 1891-1912. 13" high. *Courtesy of Dorothy & Arnold Kowalsky.*

VIENNA waste jar by Johnson Brothers, circa 1900. 13 1/2" high. *Courtesy of Joseph Nigro & Ralph Wick, Old Things Made New Again.*

WILLOW teapot by Doulton, circa 1890 with metal mounts. Printed back mark indicates this is the Royles Patent Self Pouring Teapot made for J.J. Royle by Doulton's of Burslem about 1890. The patent was granted in 1886. To pour, put your finger over the hole in the finial to create pressure and push down. The lid is of electroplated nickel silver and the cylinder, which forms the 'pump', is plated copper. Several other manufacturers produced this type of teapot. *Courtesy of Dorothy & Arnold Kowalsky.*

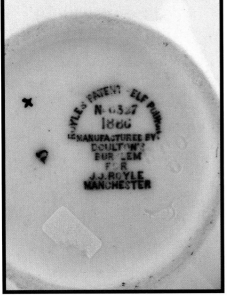

WILLOW matched sets of candlesticks by Doulton, circa 1891. *Courtesy of Dorothy & Arnold Kowalsky.*

WILLOW coffee pot for two by Doulton, with an impressed "DOULTON" mark first used in 1882. The "ENGLAND" impress begun in 1891 is not part of the mark. 7 3/8" high to the rim. *Courtesy of Dorothy & Arnold Kowalsky.*

WILLOW sauce tureen ladle by Doulton, circa 1891. *Courtesy of Dorothy & Arnold Kowalsky.*

# Bibliography

Anon. *The Ladys Companion: or, Sketches of Life, Manners, and Morals.* Philadelphia, Pennsylvania: H. C. Peck & Theo. Bliss, 1851.

*The Art Journal Illustrated Catalogue: The Industry of All Nations 1851.* London: George Virtue, 1851.

Barber, Edwin Atlee. *Marks of American Potters.* Southampton, New York: Cracker Barrel Press, n.d.

Bergesen, Victoria. *Majolica. British, Continental and American Wares 1851-1915.* London: Barrie & Jenkins, 1989.

Book Club Associates. *The Oxford Dictionary of Quotations, Third Edition.* Oxford, England: Oxford University Press, 1980.

Cable, Mary & the Editors of American Heritage. *American Manners & Morals.* New York: American Heritage Publishing Company Inc., 1969.

Cameron, Elisabeth. *Encyclopedia of Pottery & Porcelain. 1800-1960.* New York: Facts on File Publications, 1986.

Cecil, Victoria. *Minton 'Majolica.' An Historical Survey and Exhibition Catalogue.* London: Jeremy Cooper Ltd, 1982.

*The Centennial Exposition Guide 1876, Fairmount Park.* Philadelphia, Pennsylvania: Hamlin & Lawrence, 1876.

Chevalier, Michael. *Society, Manners & Politics in the United States Being a Series of Letters on North America.* Boston, Massachusetts: Weeks, Jordan & Company, 1839.

Clark, Garth. *Ceramic Art: Comment and Review 1882-1977.* New York: Dutton, 1978.

Cushion, J.P. and W.B. Honey. *Handbook of Pottery & Porcelain Marks.* London: Faber and Faber, 1980.

Dawes, Nicholas M. *Majolica.* New York: Crown Publishers, Inc., 1990.

Dean, Patricia. *The Official Identification Guide to Pottery & Porcelain.* Orlando, Florida: The House of Collectibles, Inc., 1984.

Dickens, Charles. *Pictures From Italy and American Notes.* Bloomsbury, England: The Nonesuch Press, 1938 (reprint, first published 1842).

Frederick, Gale, Valorie and Tom Hays, Ellen Hill, Lou Nelson, and Dan Overmeyer. *Flow Blue and Mulberry Teapot Body Styles.* The Flow Blue International Collectors' Club, Inc., 1993.

Gaston, Mary Frank. *The Collector's Encyclopedia of Flow Blue China.* Paducah, Kentucky: Collector Books, 1983.

Godden, Geoffrey A. *Encyclopaedia of British Pottery and Porcelain Marks.* New York: Bonanza Books, 1964.

_____, *The Concise Guide to British Pottery and Porcelain.* London: Barrie & Jenkins, 1990.

Grun, Bernard. *The Timetables of History. A Horizontal Linkage of People and Events.* New York: Simon & Schuster, Inc., 1979.

Honey, W.B. *English Pottery & Porcelain.* London: Adam & Charles Black, 1962. [new edition of 1933 original].

Hughes, Bernard and Therle. *The Collector's Encyclopaedia of English Cermaics.* London: Abbey Library, 1968.

Jewitt, Llewellynn. *The Ceramic Art of Great Britain.* Poole, Dorset, England: New Orchard Editions Ltd., 1985 [new edition from 1877 original].

Jones, Joan, *Minton. The First Two Hundred Years of Design and Production.* Swan Hill Press, 1993.

Karmason, Marilyn G. with Joan B. Stacke. *Majolica. A Complete History and Illustrated Survey.* New York: Harry N. Abrams, Inc., Publishers, 1989.

Klein, Terry H. "Nineteenth-Century Ceramics and Models of Consumer Behavior." *Historical Archaeology* 25(2), 1991.

Kovel, Ralph and Terry. *Kovels' New Dictionary of Marks. Pottery &*
*Porcelain, 1850 to the Present.* New York: Crown Publishers, 1986.

Kowalsky, Arnold, Personal papers and communications, New York, 1994.

Larkin, Jack. *The Reshaping of Everyday Life. 1790-1840.* New York: Harper & Row, Publishers, 1988.

Lehner, Lois. *Lehner's Encyclopedia of U.S. Marks on Pottery, Porcelain & Clay.* Paducah, Kentucky: Collector Books, 1988.

Little, W.L. *Staffordshire Blue. Underglaze Blue Transfer-printed Earthenware.* New York: Crown Publishers, Inc., 1969.

Miller, George L. "A Revised Set of CC Index Values for Classification and Economic Scaling of English Ceramics from 1787 to 1880." *Historical Archaeology,* Vol. 25(1), 1991.

Morison, Samuel Eliot and Henry Steele Commanger. *The Growth of the American Republic, Volume One.* New York: Oxford University Press, 1942.

Newhouse, Elizabeth L. (ed.). *The Story of America.* Washington, D.C.: National Geographic Society, 1992.

Nye, Russel Blaine. *Society and Culture in America, 1830-1860.* New York: Harper Torchbooks, Harper & Row, Publishers, 1974.

*Official Catalogue of the Great Exhibition of the Works of Industry of All Nations, 1851.* By Authority of the Royal Commission. London: W. Clowes & Sons Printers, 1852.

Panati, Charles. *Panati's Extraordinary Endings of Practically Everything and Everybody.* New York: Harper & Row, Publishers, 1989.

Pool, Daniel. *What Jane Austen Ate and Charles Dickens Knew. From Fox Hunting to Whist — the Facts of Daily Life in 19th-Century England.* New York: Simon & Schuster, 1993.

Quimby, Ian M.G. (ed.). *Material Culture and the Study of American Life. A Winterthur Book.* New York & London: W.W. Norton & Company, 1978.

*Reports by the Juries on the Subject in the Thirty Classes into Which the Exhibition Was Divided.* By Authority of the Royal Commission, Vol. III. (of four). London: W. Clowes & Sons, Printers, 1852.

Royal Doulton. *Dating Doulton. A Brief Guide.* Stoke-on-Trent, England: Royal Doulton Tableware Limited, n.d.

Rydell, Robert W. *All the World's a Fair. Visions of Empire at American International Expositions, 1876-1916.* Chicago, Illinois: The University of Chicago Press, 1984.

Savage, George and Harold Newman. *An Illustrated Dictionary of Ceramics.* London: Thames and Hudson, 1989.

Snyder, Jeffrey B., *Flow Blue. A Collector's Guide to Pattern, History, and Values.* West Chester, Pennsylvania: Schiffer Publishing Ltd., 1992.

Snyder, Jeffrey B. and Leslie Bockol. *Majolica. American & European Wares.* Atglen, Pennsylvania: Schiffer Publishing Ltd., 1994.

Wall, Diana Di Zerega. "Sacred Dinners and Secular Teas: Constructing Domesticity in Mid-19th-Century New York." *Historical Archaeology* 25(4), 1991.

Ward, Geoffrey C., Ric Burns & Ken Burns. *The Civil War. An Illustrated History.* New York: Alfred A. Knopf, Inc., 1990.

Williams, Petra. Flow *Blue China. An Aid to Identification.* Jeffersontown, Kentucky: Fountain House East, 1971.

_____. *Flow Blue China and Mulberry Ware. Similarity and Value Guide.* Jeffersontown, Kentucky. Fountain House East, 1975.

Williams, Susan. *Savory Suppers and Fashionable Feasts. Dining in Victorian America.* New York: Pantheon Books, 1985.

# Endnotes

## Chapter 1

1. George Savage, et al., *An Illustrated Dictionary of Cermaics* (London: Thames and Hudson, 1989), 251; Jeffrey B. Snyder, *Flow Blue. A Collector's Guide to Pattern, History and Values* (West Chester, Pennsylvania: Schiffer Publishing Ltd., 1992), 5 & 11.
2. Bernard and Therle Hughes, *The Collector's Encyclopaedia of English Ceramics* (London: Abbey Library, 1968), 150; Snyder, Flow Blue, 11.
3. Snyder, *Flow Blue,* 11.
4. Hughes, *The Collector's Encyclopaedia of English Ceramics,* 36; W.L. Little, *Staffordshire Blue. Underglaze Blue Transfer-printed Earthenware* (New York: Crown Publishers, Inc., 1969), 10.
5. Joan Jones, *Minton. The First Two Hundred Years of Design & Production* (Swan Hill Press, 1993), 48-49.
6. Garth Clark, *Ceramic Art: Comment & Review 1882-1977* (New York: Dutton, 1978), 84.
7. Hughes, *The Collector's Encyclopaedia of English Ceramics,* 151.
8. Snyder, *Flow Blue,* 11.
9. ibid, 16.
10. ibid, 24-25; Petra Williams, *Flow Blue China. An Aid to Identification* (Jeffersontown, Kentucky: Fountain House East, 1971), 7-8.

## Chapter 2

1. Book Club Associates, *The Oxford Dictionary of Quotations.* Third Edition. (Oxford, England: Oxford University Press, 1980), 267.
2. Nicholas M. Dawes, *Majolica* (New York: Crown Publishers, Inc., 1990), 9; Marilyn G. Karmason, et al., *Majolica. A Complete History and Illustrated Survey* (New York: Harry N. Abrams, Inc., Publishers, 1989), 11 and 13.
3. Snyder, *Flow Blue,* 8-10.
4. ibid, 12-13.
5. Jack Larkin, *The Reshaping of Everyday Life, 1790-1840* (New York: Harper and Row, Publishers, 1988), 180.
6. Samuel Eliot Morison, et al., *The Growth of the American Republic.* Volume One (New York: Oxford University Press, 1942), 494.
7. Larkin, *The Reshaping of Everyday Life, 1790-1840,* 158; Charles Dickens, *Pictures From Italy and American Notes* (Bloomsbury, England: The Nonesuch Press, 1938 [reprint]), 83.
8. Morison et al., *The Growth of the American Republic,* 493.
9. Michael Chevalier, *Society, Manners & Politics in the United States Being a Series of Letters on North America* (Boston, Massachusetts: Weeks, Jordan & Company, 1839), 82; Dickens, *Pictures From Italy and American Notes,* 59.
10. Terry H. Klein, "Nineteenth-Century Ceramics and Models of Consumer Behavoir." *Historical Archaeology* 25(2), 1991, 78-79.
11. ibid, 79; Chevalier, *Society, Manners & Politics in the United States Beings a Series of Letters on North America,* 342.
12. Klein, "Nineteenth-Century Ceramics and Models of Consumer Behavior", 79.
13. Larkin, *The Reshaping of Everyday Life, 1790-1840,* 144.
14. ibid, 160-161; Geoffrey A. Godden, *The Concise Guide to British Pottery and Porcelain* (London: Barrie & Jenkins, 1990), 187.
15. Larkin, *The Reshaping of Everyday Life, 1790-1840,* 157 & 167; Chevalier, *Society, Manners & Politics in the United States Being a Series of Letters on North America,* 83.
16. Larkin, *The Reshaping of Everyday Life, 1790-1840,* 180.
17. ibid, 180.
18. ibid, 171.
19. Daniel Pool, *What Jane Austen Ate & Charles Dickens Knew. From Fox Hunting to Whist — the Facts of Daily Life in 19th-Century England* (New York: Simon & Schuster, 1993), 205.
20. Klein, "Nineteenth-Century Ceramics and Models of Consumer Behavior", 79-80; George L. Miller, "A Revised Set of CC Index Values for Classification & Economic Scaling of English Ceramics from 1787 to 1889." *Historical Archaeology* Vol. 25(1), 1991, 1-25.
21. Larkin, *The Reshaping of Everyday Life, 1790-1840,* 174.
22. Geoffrey C. Ward, et al., *The Civil War. An Illustrated History* (New York: Alfred A. Knopf, Inc., 1990), 123.
23. Dickens, *Pictures From Italy and American Notes,* 92-93.
24. Larkin, *The Reshaping of Everyday Life, 1790-1840,* 138-139; Susan Williams, *Savory Suppers and Fashionable Feasts. Dining in Victorian America* (New York: Pantheon Books, 1985), 6; Elizabeth L. Newhouse (ed.), *The Story of America* (Washington, D.C.: National Geographic Society, 1992), 237-239.
25. Klein, "Nineteenth-Century Ceramics and Models of Consumer Behavior", 80.
26. Ian M.G. Quimby (ed.), *Material Culture and the Study of American Life* (New York & London: W.W. Norton & Company, 1978), 60-63; Mary Cable, et al., *American Manners & Morals* (New York: American Heritage Publishing Company, Inc., 1969), 216; Pool, *What Jane Austen Ate and Charles Dickens Knew,* 66.
27. Pool, *What Jane Austen Ate and Charles Dickens Knew,* 66.
28. Diana Di Zerega Wall, "Sacred Dinners and Secular Teas: Constructing Domesticity in Mid-19th-Century New York." *Historical Archaeology* 25(4), 1991, 70; Karmason, et al., *Majolica,* 141.
29. Pool, *What Jane Austen Ate and Charles Dickens Knew,* 72.
30. Miller, "A Revised Set of CC Index Values for Classification & Economic Scaling of English Ceramics from 1787 to 1889.", 1-25; Williams, *Savory Suppers and Fashionable Feasts,* 80.
31. Pool, *What Jane Austen Ate and Charles Dickens Knew,* 75.
32. Jeffrery B. Snyder & Leslie Bockol, *Majolica. American & European Wares* (Atglen, Pennsylvania: Schiffer Publishing Ltd., 1994), 54.
33. Pool, *What Jane Austen Ate and Charles Dickens Knew,* 75; Victoria Bergesen, *Majolica. British, Continental & American Wares 1851-1915* (London: Barrie & Jenkins, 1989), 22.
34. Godden, *The Concise Guide to British Pottery and Porcelain,* 80.
35. Snyder & Bockol, *Majolica,* 20.
36. Pool, *What Jane Austen Ate and Charles Dickens Knew,* 77.
37. Godden, *The Concise Guide to British Pottery and Porcelain,* 80-81.
38. ibid, 80.
39. Anonymous, *The Ladys Companion: or, Sketches of Life, Manners, & Morals* (Philadephia, Pennsylvania: H.C. Peck & Theo. Bliss, 1851), 15-16.
40. ibid, 16.
41. Williams, *Savory Suppers and Fashionable Feasts,* 79-80.
42. Bergesen, *Majolica,* 11.
43. ibid, 10-11.
44. ibid, 11; Dawes, *Majolica,* 154-155.
45. Bergesen, *Majolica,* 11.
46. *Reports by the Juries on the Subject in the Thirty Classes into Which the Exhibition Was Divided* (London: W. Clowes & Sons, Printers, 1852), 1190.
47. ibid, 1189.
48. Dawes, *Majolica,* 155.
49. ibid, 155.
50. *The Centennial Exposition Guide 1876, Fairmount Park* (Philadelphia, Pennsylvania: Hamlin & Lawrence, 1876), 1.
51. ibid, 1; Robert W. Rydell, *All the World's a Fair. Visions of Empire at American International Expositions, 1876-1916* (Chicago, Illinois: The University of Chicago Press, 1984), 10.
52. *The Centennial Exposition Guide 1876, Fairmount Park,* 19.
53. Edwin Atlee Barber, *Marks of American Potters* (Southampton, New York: Cracker Barrel Press, n.d.).
54. Patricia Dean, *The Official Identification Guide to Pottery & Porcelain* (Orlando, Florida: The House of Collectibles, Inc., 1984), 266.
55. Russel Blaine Nye, *Society & Culture in America, 1830-1860* (New York: Harper Torchbooks, Harper & Row Publishers, 1974), 159, 172-173.
56. Nye, *Society & Culture in America, 1830-1860,* 181.
57. Charles Panati, *Panati's Extraordinary Endings of Practically Everything & Everybody* (New York: Harper & Row, Publishers, 1989), 30.
58. Victoria Cecil, *Minton 'Majolica.' An Historical Survey & Exhibition Catalogue* (London: Jeremy Cooper Ltd., 1982), 22; Snyder & Bockol, *Majolica,* 77.
59. Bergesen, *Majolica,* 17.
60. *The Art Journal Illustrated Catalogue: The Industry of All Nations 1851* (London: George Virtue, 1851), 240.
61. Snyder & Bockol, *Majolica,* 86.
62. Dawes, *Majolica,* 56.
63. Dean, *The Official Identification Guide to Pottery & Porcelain,* 266; W.B. Honey, *English Pottery & Porcelain* (London: Adam & Charles Black, 1962).

## Chapter 3

1. Llewellynn Jewitt, *The Ceramic Art of Great Britain* (Poole, Dorset, England: New Orchard Editions Ltd., 1985 [reprint of 1877 edition]), 381; Dawes, *Majolica,* 134-135.
2. Godden, *The Concise Guide to British Pottery and Porcelain,* 15-16.
3. Elisabeth Cameron, *Encyclopedia of Pottery & Porcelain. 1800-1960* (New York: Facts on File Publications, 1986), 9; Godden, *The Concise Guide to British Pottery and Porcelain,* 22; Geoffrey A. Godden, *Encyclopaedia of British Pottery & Porcelain Marks* (New York: Bonanza Books, 1964), 20-22 *this valuable source was used throughout the marks in text and captions; Hughes, *The Collector's Encyclopaedia of English Ceramics,* 11; Jewitt, *The Ceramic Art of Great Britain,* 423, 432, 464 & 497.
4. Godden, *The Concise Guide to British Pottery and Porcelain,* 22-23; Hughes, *The Collector's Encyclopaedia of English Ceramics,* 12-13; Jewitt, *The Ceramic Art of Great Britain,* 459.
5. Jewitt, *The Ceramic Art of Great Britain,* 491-492.
6. ibid, 497-499.
7. Cameron, *Encyclopedia of Pottery & Porcelain. 1800-1960,* 64; Dawes, *Majolica,* 131; Godden, *The Concise Guide to British Pottery and Porcelain,* 51.
8. Dawes, *Majolica,* 134; Godden, *The Concise Guide to British Pottery and Porcelain,* 49-50; Jewitt, *The Ceramic Art of Great Britain,* 472.
9. Jewitt, *The Ceramic Art of Great Britain,* 461.
10. Godden, *The Concise Guide to British Pottery and Porcelain,* 57.
11. Jewitt, *The Ceramic Art of Great Britain,* 554.
12. ibid, 499-500.
13. *The Art Journal Illustrated Catalogue: The Industry of All Nations 1851,* 1; Dawes, *Majolica,* 123; Godden, *The Concise Guide to British Pottery and Porcelain,* 66-67; Jewitt, *The Ceramic Art of Great Britain,* 381-390.
14. Godden, *The Concise Guide to British Pottery and Porcelain,* 74; Jewitt, *The Ceramic Art of Great Britain,* 467-469; Hughes, *The Collector's Encyclopaedia of English Ceramics.*
15. *Reports by the Juries on the Subject in the Thirty Classes into Which the Exhibition Was Divided,* 1190; *Official Catalogue of the Great Exhibition of the Works of Industry of All Nations, 1851* (London: W. Clowes & Sons Printers, 1852), 129; Jewitt, *The Ceramic Art of Great Britain,* 501.
16. Cameron, *Encyclopedia of Pottery & Porcelain. 1800-1960,* 111-114; Jewitt, *The Ceramic Art of Great Britain,* 448-450; Royal Doulton, *Dating Doulton. A Brief Guide* (Stoke-on-Trent, England: Royal Doulton Tableware Limited, n.d.), 3-11.
17. Jewitt, *The Ceramic Art of Great Britain,* 456-457.
18. Godden, *Encyclopaedia of British Pottery & Porcelain Marks,* 245; *Official Catalogue of the Great Exhibition of the Works of Industry of All Nations, 1851,* 129.
19. Godden, *Encyclopaedia of British Pottery & Porcelain Marks,* 262-264; Jewitt, *The Ceramic Art of Great Britain,* 476-477.
20. Godden, *Encyclopaedia of British Pottery & Porcelain Marks,* 294.
21. ibid, 355-356.
22. ibid, 405-407; Jewitt, *The Ceramic Art of Great Britain,* 458.
23. Jewitt, *The Ceramic Art of Great Britain,* 451-456; *Official Catalogue of the Great Exhibition of the Works of Industry of All Nations, 1851,* 129; *Reports by the Juries on the Subject in the Thirty Classes into Which the Exhibition Was Divided,* 1190.
24. Godden, *Encyclopaedia of British Pottery & Porcelain Marks,* 425-427; Jewitt, *The Ceramic Art of Great Britain,* 566.
25. *The Art Journal Illustrated Catalogue: The Industry of All Nations, 1851,* 240; Cameron, *Encyclopedia of Pottery & Porcelain. 1800-1960,* 220; Godden, *The Concise Guide to British Pottery and Porcelain,* 125; Jewitt, *The Ceramic Art of Great Britain,* 488-491.
26. Cameron, *Encyclopedia of Pottery & Porcelain. 1800-1960,* 226-227; Dawes, *Majolica,* 80, 86; Godden, *The Concise Guide to British Pottery and Porcelain,* 127; Hughes, *The Collector's Encyclopaedia of English Ceramics;* Jewitt, *The Ceramic Art of Great Britain,* 408-409, 413; Jones, *Minton.* (Swan Hill Press, 1993), 48-49; *Official Catalogue of the Great Exhibition of the Works of Industry of All Nations, 1851,* 129.
27. Godden, *Encyclopaedia of British Pottery & Porcelain Marks,* 467.
28. Cameron, *Encyclopedia of Pottery & Porcelain. 1800-1960,* 263; Jewitt, *The Ceramic Art of Great Britain,* 565.
29. Godden, *Encyclopaedia of British Pottery & Porcelain Marks,* 501.
30. *The Art Journal Illustrated Catalogue: The Industry of All Nations 1851,* 86-87; Godden, *The Concise Guide to British Pottery and Porcelain,* 152-153; Hughes, *The Collector's Encyclopaedia of English Ceramics,* 128; Jewitt, *The Ceramic Art of Great Britain,* 492-496; *Official Catalogue of the Great Exhibition of the Works of Industry of All Nations, 1851,* 129; *Reports by the Juries on the Subject in the Thirty Classes into Which the Exhibition Was Divided,* 1189-1190.
31. Cameron, *Encyclopedia of Pottery & Porcelain. 1800-1960,* 349; Dawes, *Majolica,* 93, 108; Godden, *The Concise Guide to British Pottery and Porcelain,* 187-188; Jewitt, *The Ceramic Art of Great Britain,* 562-563; *Reports by the Juries on the Subject in the Thirty Classes into Which the Exhibition Was Divided,* 1189.
32. *Reports by the Juries on the Subject in the Thirty Classes into Which the Exhibition Was Divided,* 1189.
33. Snyder & Bockol, *Majolica,* 48.
34. Barber, *Marks of American Potters,* 58.
35. Lois Lehner, *Lehner's Encyclopedia of U.S. Marks on Pottery, Porcelain & Clay* (Paducah, Kentucky: Collector Books, 1988), 100.
36. Barber, *Marks of American Potters,* 135; Lehner, *Lehner's Encyclopedia of U.S. Marks on Pottery, Porcelain & Clay,* 155.
37. Barber, *Marks of American Potters,* 33; Lehner, *Lehner's Encyclopedia of U.S. Marks on Pottery, Porcelain & Clay,* 283.
38. Barber, *Marks of American Potters,* 57; Cameron, *Encyclopedia of Pottery & Porcelain. 1800-1960,* 222; Lehner, *Lehner's Encyclopedia of U.S. Marks on Pottery, Porcelain & Clay,* 293.
39. Lehner, *Lehner's Encyclopedia of U.S. Marks on Pottery, Porcelain & Clay,* 414.
40. ibid.
41. Barber, *Marks of American Potters,* 149; Cameron, *Encyclopedia of Pottery & Porcelain. 1800-1960,* 352.
42. Dawes, *Majolica,* 138.
43. ibid, 146.
44. ibid, 152.

## Chapter 4

1. Bernard Grun, *The Timetables of History. A Horizontal Linkage of People and Events* (New York: Simon & Schuster, Inc., 1979), 400-424.
2. Grun, *The Timetables of History,* 400-424.
3. ibid, 424-429.
4. ibid, 429-439.
5. ibid, 439-453.
6. ibid, 453-457.

## Appendix

1. Arnold Kowalsky, *Personal papers,* New York, 1994.

# Appendix

The following is a survey of Flow Blue manufacturers, their patterns and their periods of production.[1]

## Potters & Patterns of the Early & Mid-Victorian Period c. 1835-1870

| POTTER | DATE | PATTERN | GODDEN NO. | POTTER | DATE | PATTERN | GODDEN NO |
|--------|------|---------|-----------|--------|------|---------|-----------|
| Wm. Adams & Sons | 1819-64 | Tonquin | 22 | Joseph Heath | 1845-53 | Tonquin | 1993 |
| Samuel Alcock | 1828-59 | Carlton | 75 | John Maddock & Sons | 1855-Pres. | Hindustan | 2461 |
| Sam.Alcock & Co. | 1828-59 | Oriental | 75 | T.J.&J. Mayer | 1843-55 | Arabesque | 2570 |
| J&G Alcock | 1839-46 | Scinde | 69 | T.J.&J. Mayer | 1843-55 | Oregon | 2570 |
| Alcock (?) | - | Sobraon | - | Charles Meigh | 1835-49 | Hong Kong | 2618 |
| Edw. Challinor | 1842-67 | Kin-Shan | 836 | Charles Meigh | 1835-49 | Indian | 2617 |
| Edw. Challinor | 1842-67 | Pelew | 835A | Charles Meigh | 1835-49 | Troy | 2614A/2618 |
| Edw. Challinor | 1842-67 | Shell | 835 | John Meir | 1812-36 | Chen-Si | 2632 |
| Jos. Clementson | 1839-64 | Chusan | 910A | John Meir & Sons | 1837-97 | Kirkee | 2639 |
| Wm. Davenport & Co. | 1844 | Amoy | 1181A | John Meir & Sons | 1837-97 | Kyber | 2639 |
| Thos. Dimmock | 1828-59 | Bamboo | 1298 | Ridgway & Morley | 1842-44 | Cashmere | 3278 |
| Thos. Dimmock | 1828-59 | Chinese | 1298 | Francis Morley & Co. | 1845-58 | Cashmere | 2760 |
| Thos. Dimmock | 1828-59 | Mandarin | 1298 | Wm. Ridgway | 1830-34 | Formosa | 3301 |
| Thos. Dimmock | 1828-59 | Pekin | 1299 | Mellor Venables & Co. | 1834-51 | Beauties of China | 2645 |
| James Edwards | 1842-51 | Canton | 1455 | Podmore Walker | 1834-59 | Kaolin | 3075 |
| John Edwards | 1847-74 | Coburg | 1449 | Podmore Walker | 1834-59 | Manila | 3075 |
| John Edwards & Co. | 1873-79 | Coburg | 1450 | Thos. Walker | 1845-51 | Nankin | 3982 |
| Thos. Fell & Co. | 1830-90 | Japan | 1534 | Podmore Walker | 1849-59 | Temple | 3080 |
| Jacob Furnival | 1845-70 | Gothic | 1643 | John Wedgwood | 1841-60 | Chapoo | 4276A |
| Jacob Furnival | 1845-70 | Shanghae | 1643 | John Wedgwood | 1840-45 | Chusan | 4075 |
| Jac. & Thos. Furnival | 1843 | Indian Jar | 1644 | John Wedgwood | 1840-45 | Chusan | 4085 |
| Thos. Furnival & Co. | 1844-46 | Rhone | 1645 | John Wedgwood | 1840-68 | Chusan | 4086 |
| Wm. Hackwood | 1827-55 | Rhoda Gardens | 1860 | | | | |

## Potters & Patterns of the Late Victorian Period c. 1880s-20th Century

| POTTER | PATTERN | DATE MANUFACTURED | YEARS POTTER IN BUSINESS | REGISTRY NO. | GODDEN REF. NO |
|--------|---------|-------------------|--------------------------|--------------|----------------|
| William Adams & Co. | Fairy Villas | 1893-1917 | 1819-Present | - | 31 |
| | Kyber | " | | - | 31 |
| Henry Alcock & Co. | Grenada | 1880-1910 | 1861-1910 | - | 65 |
| | Manhattan | " | | - | 65 |
| | Touraine | 1898 | | 329815 | 65 |
| Burgess & Leigh (Ltd) | Non Pareil | 1889-1910 | 1867-Present | - | 719 |
| | Vermont | 1894 | | 236650 | 717 |
| Doulton & Co. (Ltd) | Madras | 1882-1930 | 1882-Present | - | 1332-34/37/51 |
| | Watteau | " | | - | 1328 |
| French China Co. (American) | La Francaise | c.1900-1929 | - | - | Thorn.P.26, Mk.24 |
| Ford & Sons (Ltd) | Florida | c.1893-1929 | c.1893-1938 | - | 1585 |
| W.H. Grindley & Co. (Ltd) | Alaska | 1880-1924 | 1880-1960 | - | 1842 |
| | Albany | - | | | 1842 |
| | Argyle | 1896 | | 289457 | 1842 |
| | Ashburton | - | | - | 1842 |
| | Baltic | - | | - | 1842 |
| | Beaufort | 1903 | | 408448 | 1842 |
| | Blue Rose | - | | - | 1842 |
| | Clarence | - | | - | 1842 |
| | Clover | - | | - | 1843 |
| | Dutchess | 1891 | | 184838 | 1842 |
| | Florida | - | | - | 1842 |
| | Gironde | - | | | 1842 |
| | Grace | 1897 | | 303495 | 1842 |
| | Haddon | - | | - | 1842 |
| | Hofburg (The) | - | | - | 1842 |
| | Idris | - | | - | 1842 |
| | Keele | - | | - | 1842 |
| | Le Pavot | 1896 | | 277089 | 1842 |
| | Lorne | - | | - | 1842 |
| | Lotus | - | | - | 1843 |
| | Marechal Neil | 1895 | | 263030 | 1842 |

| POTTER | PATTERN | DATE MANUFACTURED | YEARS POTTER IN BUSINESS | REGISTRY NO. | GODDEN REF. NO |
|---|---|---|---|---|---|
| | Marguerite | - | | - | 1842 |
| | Marie | 1895 | | 250387 | 1842 |
| | Marquis (The) | 1906 | | 473313 | 1843 |
| | Melbourne | - | | - | 1842&1843 |
| | Osborne | - | | - | 1842 |
| | Poppy | - | | - | 1842 |
| | Portman | - | | - | 1842 |
| | Rose | 1893 | | 213117 | 1842 |
| | Shanghai | - | | - | 1842 |
| Johnson Bros. (Ltd) | Blue Danube | - | 1883-Present | - | 2177 |
| | Clarissa | - | | - | 2177 |
| | Clayton | 1902 (Oct.24) | | - | 2177 |
| | Eclipse | - | | - | 2177 |
| | Florida | - | | - | 2177 |
| | Georgia | - | | - | 2179 |
| | Holland | 1891 (?) | 1883-Present | - | 2179 |
| | Jewel | - | | - | 2177 |
| | Kenworth | - | | - | 2179 |
| | Mongolia | - | | - | 2179 |
| | Normandy | - | | - | 2177 |
| | Oxford | - | | - | 2177 |
| | Peach | - | | - | 2177 |
| | Richmond | - | | - | 2177 |
| | Savoy | - | | - | 2177 |
| | Stanley | - | | Reg.date 11/7/1898 | 2177 |
| | Warwick | - | | - | 2177 |
| George Jones (& Sons Ltd) | Abbey | 1891+ | 1864-1951 | - | - |
| John Maddock & Sons (Ltd) | Hamilton | 1880+ | 1855-Present | - | 2464 |
| | Roseville | " | | - | 2463 |
| | Virginia | " | | - | 2463 |
| | Waverly | " | | - | 2463 |
| Alfred Meakin (Ltd) | Cambridge | 1891-1930 | 1875-Present | - | 2586 |
| | Devon | " | | - | 2587 |
| | Kelvin | " | | - | 2585 |
| | Richmond | " | | - | 2586 |
| | Verona | " | | - | 2586 |
| J&G Meakin (Ltd) | Colonial | 1890+ | 1851-Present | - | 2600/2602 |
| Mercer Pottery Co. (Trenton, NJ) | Paisley | c.1868 | | - | Hartman Mk 7, p. 116 |
| New Wharf Pottery Co. | Conway | 1890-94 | 1878-1894 | - | 2886 |
| | Knox | " | | - | 2886 |
| | Lancaster | " | | - | 2886 |
| | Waldorf | " | | - | 2886 |
| Wm. Ridgway Son & Co. | Lonsdale | 1891-1920 | 1838-1952 | - | 3313 |
| | Lugano | " | | - | 3313 |
| | Oriental | " | | - | 3316 |
| | Osborne | " | | - | 3312 |
| Stanley Pottery (Ltd) | Touraine | 1928-31 | 1903-1931 | 32815 Reg.date 1898 | |
| Upper Hanley Pottery Co. (Ltd) | Muriel | 1895-1900 | 1895-1910 | - | 3928 |
| Upsala-Ekeby CELFE (Sweden) | Vinranka | (?) | to 4/23/67 | - | - |
| Utzschneider & Co. (French) | Persian Moss | - | c.1891-? | - | Hartman Mk 6, p.74 |
| Warwick China Co. (Wheeling, WV) | Warwick Pansy | - | 1887-1898 | - | Thorn Mk 38, p.152 |
| Wheeling Pottery (Wheeling, WV) | La Belle | - | 1879-1910 | - | Thorn Mk 28, p.154 |
| Arthur J. Wilkinson (Ltd) | Iowa | c.1907 | 1885-present | - | 4170 |
| F. Winkle & Co. (Ltd) | Togo | - | 1890-1930 | - | 4215 |
| Wood & Son(s)(Ltd) | Lakewood | 1891-1907 | 1865-Present | 348700 Reg.date 1899 | 4285 |
| | Seville | " | | - | 4285 |
| | Trent | " | | - | 4285 |

Values vary immensely according to the condition of the piece, the location of the market, and the overall quality of the design and manufacture. Condition is always of paramount importance in assigning a value. Prices in the Midwest differ from those in the West or East, and those at specialty antique shows will vary from those at general shows. And, of course, being at the right place at the right time can make all the difference.

All these factors make it impossible to create an absolutely accurate price list, but we can offer a guide. The prices reflect what one could realistically expect to pay at retail or auction.

The left hand number is the page number. The letters following it indicate the position of the photograph on the page: T=top, L=left, R=right, TL=top left, TR=top right, C=center, CL=center left, CR=center right, B=bottom, BL=bottom left, BR=bottom right. Sequential numbers following immediately after these letters indicate the position of the piece in a series of pieces reading from left to right or top to bottom. The right hand column of numbers are the estimated price ranges in United States dollars.

| Page | Pos | Price | Page | Pos | Price | Page | Pos | Price |
|---|---|---|---|---|---|---|---|---|
| 4 | C 1 | 430-475 | | CR | 385-315 | 57 | TR 1 | 70-80 |
| | C 2 | 950-1050 | 26 | TL | 240-260 ea. | | TR 2 | 105-115 |
| | C 3 | 140-160 | | TR | 70-80 ea. | | TR 3 | 120-130 |
| | C 4 | 475-525 | | CL | 1140-1260 | | TR 4 | 45-55 |
| | C 5 | 90-100 | | B 1 | 855-945 set | | TR 5 | 135-145 |
| 5 | TL | 525-575 | | B 2 | 380-420 set | | TR 6 | 70-80 |
| | CL | 1000-1100 | | B 3 | 475-525 set | | CR | 470-520 |
| | CR | 500-575 ea. | 27 | CL | 810-890 set | 59 | CR | 1330-1470 |
| 6 | TL | 425-475 | | CR | 760-840 set | | BR | 905-995 |
| | CR 1 | 75-85 | | B | 165-185 ea. | 61 | CL | 570-630 |
| | CR 2 | 120-130 | 28 | T | 1900-2100 | | BL | 240-260 |
| | BL | 140-160 ea. | | C | 430-470 | 62 | TR | 1710-1890 |
| 7 | TL | 45-55 ea. | | B | 525-575 | | BR | 525-575 |
| | CR | 2660-2940 set | 29 | T | 2375-2625 | 64 | TL 1 | 620-685 |
| 8 | CL | 2280-2520 | | CL | 310-345 | | TL 2 | 1140-1260 |
| 10 | TL | 2375-2625 | | CR | 1425-1575 | | CL | 215-235 |
| | TR | 1710-1890 | 30 | TL | 475-525 | 65 | BL | 85-95 |
| | BR | 135-145 | | CL | 240-260 | 66 | BR | 405-445 |
| 11 | TL | 640-710 | | CR | 355-395 | 68 | CL | 260-290 |
| | CR | 710-790 | | BL | 905-995 | 69 | TL | 335-370 |
| 12 | CL | 620-680 | 31 | TR | 390-420 | | BL | 335-370 |
| 13 | TL | 165-185 | | C | 310-340 ea. | 70 | BR | 525-575 |
| | TR | 525-575 | 32 | T | 1520-1680 | 71 | CR | 525-575 |
| | BL | 1235-1365 | | CR | 1330-1470 | | BR | 1710-1890 |
| | CR | 430-475 | | BL | 620-685 | 72 | TL | 430-475 |
| 14 | CL | 570-630 ea. | 33 | T | 1900-2100 | | CR | 260-290 |
| | BR | 1140-1260 | | C | 285-315 | 73 | B | 335-370 |
| 15 | TL | 1235-1365 | 34 | C 1 | 810-895 | 74 | TR | 620-680 |
| | TR | 1710-1890 | | C 2 | 1520-1680 | | BL | 715-790 |
| | CL 1 | 1900-2100 | 36 | T | 1900-2100 | 75 | TL | 1140-1260 |
| | CL 2 | 3325-3675 | | BL | 240-260 | | C | 2850-3150 set |
| | CR | 1140-1260 | | BR | 120-130 | | B | 760-840 ea. |
| | BL | 810-895 ea. | 37 | C | 240-265 | 76 | T 1 | 145-160 |
| 16 | TL | 380-420 ea. | | BR | 335-370 | | T 2 | 335-370 |
| | TR | 760-840 | 38 | TL | 1710-1890 | | T 3 | 145-160 |
| | BR | 1140-1260 | | BR | 165-185 | | CL | 145-160 ea. |
| 17 | TL | 1900-2100 | 39 | TR | 260-290 | | CR | 620-685 |
| | CR | 665-735 | | CL | 525-575 | | BL | 380-420 |
| | BR 1 | 285-315 | 40 | C | 285-315 | 77 | T | 925-1025 |
| | BR 2 | 380-420 | | B | 260-290 | | C | 570-630 |
| | BR 3 | 380-420 | 41 | B | 1235-1365 | 79 | TR | 1710-1890 |
| | BR 4 | 475-525 | 42 | CR | 1425-1575 | | CR | 665-735 |
| 18 | TL | 225-575 | 43 | CL | 715-790 | | BL | 335-370 |
| | TR | 855-945 | | BL | 405-445 | 80 | TL | 665-735 |
| | C | 2850-3150 | 44 | CL | 620-680 | | TR | 880-970 |
| | BR | 525-575 | 45 | CL | 525-575 | | B | 570-630 |
| 19 | TR | 85-95 | | CR | 285-315 | 81 | CL | 525-575 |
| | BL | 2850-3150 | 46 | TR | 75-85 | | BR | 620-670 |
| 20 | T | 1900-2100 | 47 | CL | 1425-1575 | 82 | TL | 715-790 |
| | C | 665-735 | | BL | 235-260 | | CL | 855-945 |
| | B | 715-785 | 48 | CL | 240-260 | | BR | 640-710 |
| 21 | TL | 1900-2100 | | CR | 855-945 | 83 | TL | 1900-2100 |
| | CR | 1710-1890 | 49 | BL | 145-155 | | TR | 145-155 |
| | BL | 1900-2100 | 50 | TL | 525-575 | | CL | 810-895 |
| 22 | T | 1520-1680 | | BL | 140-160 | | BR | 690-760 |
| | C | 475-525 | 51 | BL | 715-785 | 84 | TL | 1140-1260 |
| | B | 1045-1155 | 52 | CL | 430-470 | | TR | 620-685 |
| 23 | TL | 905-995 set | | CR | 355-395 | | CR | 125-135 |
| | TR | 475-525 | 53 | CL | 380-420 | 85 | TL | 2375-2625 |
| | CL | 285-315 | 54 | TR | 330-370 | | CL | 240-265 |
| 24 | T | 335-365 | | CL | 1995-2205 | | BL | 85-95 |
| | B | 1615-1785 | 55 | TL | 905-995 | 86 | TL | 1710-1890 |
| 25 | TL | 335-365 | | CL | 375-415 | | TR | 1140-1260 |
| | TR | 2280-2520 | 56 | TR | 145-160 | | BL | 545-605 |
| | CL | 525-575 | | BL | 355-395 | 87 | TL | 810-895 |

| No. | Pos | Value |
|---|---|---|
|  | BR | 380-420 |
| 88 | TL | 760-840 |
|  | C | 810-895 |
|  | BR | 1425-1575 |
| 89 | TL | 1330-1470 |
|  | CR | 1330-1470 |
|  | BL | 215-235 |
| 90 | T | 335-370 |
|  | CL | 525-575 |
|  | BR | 430-470 |
| 91 | TL | 715-785 |
|  | TR | 475-525 |
|  | CL | 1425-1575 |
|  | BR | 190-210 |
| 92 | TL | 310-340 |
|  | C | 665-735 |
| 93 | TL | 665-735 |
|  | CL | 665-700 |
|  | CR | 1710-1890 |
|  | BL | 380-420 |
| 94 | TL | 240-260 ea. |
|  | C | 2375-2625 |
| 95 | T | 240-260 |
|  | B | 285-315 |
| 96 | TL | 190-210 |
|  | CL | 430-470 |
|  | BL | 665-735 ea. |
| 97 | TR | 240-260 |
|  | CR | 1900-2100 |
|  | BR | 855-945 |
| 98 | TR | 1615-1785 |
|  | CR | 355-395 |
|  | BR | 2850-3150 |
| 99 | TL | 2850-3150 |
|  | CL 1 | 240-260 |
|  | CL 2 | 45-55 |
|  | CL 3 | 240-260 |
|  | BL | 150-170 |
| 100 | TL | 475-525 |
|  | TR | 355-395 |
|  | BL | 810-890 |
|  | BR | 380-420 |
| 101 | TL | 380-420 |
|  | TR | 525-575 |
|  | BL | 145-155 |
|  | BR | 405-445 |
| 102 | TL | 665-735 |
|  | CL | 180-200 |
|  | BR | 570-630 |
| 103 | TL | 120-130 |
|  | TR | 715-790 |
|  | BL | 905-1000 |
|  | BR | 335-370 |
| 104 | TL | 475-525 |
|  | C | 715-790 |
|  | BR | 810-890 |
| 105 | T | 165-185 ea. |
|  | B 1 | 285-315 |
|  | B 2 | 855-945 |
| 106 | TR | 1045-1155 |
|  | CR | 430-475 |
|  | BR | 1425-1575 |
| 107 | TL | 335-370 |
|  | CR | 160-180 |
|  | BR 1 | 905-1000 |
|  | BR 2 | 1045-1155 |
| 109 | C | 170-190 |
| 110 |  | 715-790 |
| 112 | TL | 145-155 |
|  | CR | 620-685 |
|  | BL | 620-685 |
| 113 | T | 545-605 |
|  | C 1 | 810-895 |
|  | C 2 | 430-475 |
| 115 | T 1 | 145-155 |
|  | T 2 | 215-235 |

| No. | Pos | Value |
|---|---|---|
|  | T 3 | 145-155 |
|  | CL | 355-395 |
| 116 | TL | 1140-1260 |
|  | TR | 145-155 |
| 117 | TL | 855-945 |
|  | CL | 2660-2940 |
|  | BL | 620-680 |
| 118 | TL | 1900-2100 |
|  | CL 1 | 260-290 |
|  | CL 2 | 470-520 |
| 119 | TL | 430-475 |
|  | BL | 1900-2100 |
|  | BR | 760-840 |
| 120 | TL | 475-525 |
|  | CL | 165-185 |
|  | BR | 430-475 |
| 121 | TL | 1425-1575 |
|  | CL | 620-685 |
|  | BL | 355-395 |
|  | TL 2 | 285-315 |
| 122 | CR | 715-790 |
|  | BL | 430-475 |
| 123 | TL | 715-790 |
|  | TR | 560-620 |
|  | CR | 620-685 |
|  | BL 1 | 570-630 |
|  | BL 2 | 665-735 |
|  | BL 3 | 570-630 |
|  | TL | 55-65 |
| 124 | CL | 1710-1890 |
|  | BL | 1140-1260 |
| 125 | TR | 760-840 |
|  | CR | 1330-1470 |
|  | BR | 1615-1785 |
| 126 | TL | 810-890 |
|  | CL | 145-155 |
|  | CR | 180-200 |
| 127 | TL | 145-155 |
|  | CR | 285-315 |
|  | BL | 1520-1680 |
| 128 | C | 715-790 |
| 129 | TL | 620-685 |
|  | TR | 620-685 |
|  | B | 905-995 |
| 130 | TL | 525-575 |
|  | TR | 335-370 |
| 131 | TL | 355-395 |
|  | BL | 380-420 |
| 132 | CL | 240-260 |
|  | BR | 190-210 |
| 133 | TL | 145-155 |
|  | CL | 310-340 |
|  | CR | 240-260 |
|  | BR | 810-895 |
| 134 | TL | 310-340 |
|  | CL | 180-200 |
|  | BR | 145-155 |
| 135 | TL | 285-315 ea. |
|  | CL | 570-630 |
|  | BR | 285-315 |
| 136 | TL | 430-475 |
|  | TR | 855-945 |
|  | CL | 430-475 ea. |
|  | BR | 280-310 |
| 137 | TL | 275-305 |
|  | CL | 165-185 |
|  | BL | 430-475 |
| 138 | TL | 405-445 |
|  | TR | 335-370 |
| 139 | TL | 430-475 |
|  | CR | 620-670 |
|  | BL | 450-495 |
| 141 | BR | 240-260 |
| 142 | TR/BR | 335-370 |
| 143 | T/B | 335-370 |
| 144 | TL | 285-315 |

| No. | Pos | Value |
|---|---|---|
|  | TR | 260-290 |
|  | BL | 355-395 |
| 145 | TL | 715-790 |
|  | TR/BR | 1520-1680 |
| 146 | TL | 335-370 |
|  | CL | 285-315 |
|  | BL | 355-395 |
| 147 | TL | 1140-1260 |
|  | CL | 145-155 |
|  | BR | 80-90 |
| 148 | TL | 855-945 |
|  | TR | 120-130 |
|  | CL | 665-735 |
|  | CR | 240-260 |
|  | BL | 70-80 |
| 149 | TL 1 | 45-55 |
|  | TL 2 | 35-45 |
|  | TL 3 | 35-45 |
|  | CR | 430-475 |
|  | B 1 | 40-60 |
|  | B 2 | 40-60 |
|  | B 3 | 90-100 |
|  | B 4 | 90-100 |
|  | B 5 | 120-130 |
| 150 | TL 1 | 165-185 |
|  | TL 2 | 120-130 |
|  | TL 3 | 120-130 |
|  | CR | 1140-1260 |
|  | BL | 1140-1260 |
| 151 | TR 1 | 260-285 |
|  | TR 2 | 190-210 |
|  | TR 3 | 260-285 |
|  | CL 1 | 145-155 |
|  | CL 2 | 165-185 |
|  | CL 3 | 145-155 |
|  | BR | 380-420 |
| 152 | T/C | 2850-3150 |
|  | B | 1805-1995 |
| 153 | TL | 285-315 |
|  | CL | 260-290 |
|  | BL | 165-185 |
|  | BR | 260-290 |
| 154 | TL | 620-685 |
|  | CL | 500-550 |
|  | BR | 275-305 |
| 155 | TL | 35-45 |
|  | TR | 15-25 |
|  | B | 620-685 |
| 156 | TL | 280-310 |
|  | CR | 570-630 |
|  | BL | 525-575 |
| 157 | B 1 | 240-260 |
|  | B 2 | 70-80 |
|  | B 3 | 240-260 |
| 158 | TL | 165-185 |
|  | CL | 165-185 |
|  | CR | 55-65 |
|  | BL | 215-235 |
| 159 | TL | 380-420 |
|  | TR | 1140-1260 |
|  | CR | 240-260 |
|  | BL | 55-65 |
| 160 |  | 165-185 |
| 161 |  | 275-305 |
| 162 | CL | 205-445 |
|  | BR | 570-630 |
| 163 | BL | 275-305 |
| 164 | T | 430-475 |
|  | BL | 830-920 |
| 165 | TL | 620-685 |
|  | BR | 760-840 |
| 166 |  | 525-575 |
| 167 |  | 570-630 |
| 168 | TL | 570-630 |
|  | BR | 285-315 |

# Index